No Fault No Blame

Channeled support and encouragement for trauma survivors

Channeled by River Lightbearer

In collaboration with Shiva and Pietkela, beings of light

Cover by Kim Ramsey-Winkler

Published by:

Vegan Wolf Productions

veganwolfproductions@gmail.com

Contents

River's Introduction: Why This Book?

J grew up in, to put it lightly, a difficult environment. I was frequently afraid, often felt like I couldn't do anything right or worthwhile, and the adults around me, struggling with their own pasts, didn't always care for or protect me the way a child needs to be cared for and protected.

Enter my guides.

When I was about two years old, invisible beings started speaking with me. They gave me the care, love, and protection I craved, along with suggestions of beneficial ways to handle things and sometimes just fun and jokes. When I asked their names, they gave responses that were related to things I understood at the time, like TV shows or church. Although I couldn't see them, they were very real to me, and I was quick to correct anyone who referred to them as my imaginary friends. They weren't imaginary, just invisible.

As I got older, the experiences I had at home, with other family members, and at school became more damaging. I was bullied by peers and emotionally and verbally abused by family members and caretakers, and I developed the impression that all of this happened because I somehow deserved it. I learned to be constantly on guard whenever anyone was nearby in case something bad happened. I learned to perceive almost everyone and everything as threats. Except my invisible friends.

That perception of the world and all it includes as threats is part of post-traumatic stress disorder. This book is not about PTSD or complex-PTSD in general. I'm not a licensed professional, and my knowledge on the subject comes from study, research, and personal experiences. If you want to learn more about PTSD and CPTSD, I strongly recommend Bessel van Der Kolk's book *The Body Keeps the Score*. I'll list other resources at the end of this book.

This book, however, isn't about trauma. It isn't about what I've lived through, even though my experiences and my knowledge about trauma is what spurred me to write this.

Throughout my life, those invisible beings, whom I now know as my guides, have been with me. They've offered me support and compassion. They've shown me love when I wasn't able to feel any for myself. They've given me a nonhuman perspective on human experiences, why we do what we do to ourselves and one another. And they've guided me through the trauma and into my healing journey.

In August 2020, I started channeling daily messages from my guide Shiva, a being of light, to post on my Facebook business page and personal profile. A number of those messages reference trauma and the healing journey.

Shiva has been with me for as long as I can remember, though I haven't always known him by that name. For a number of years, because of my experiences, my energetic vibration dropped too low for Shiva to safely interact with me in a direct manner, but even then he was with me, interacting with me through my spirit guide Dominic.

Dominic acted as an intermediary until 2006, when, through healing work I did on my own and with my mentor, my vibration returned to a level at which direct interaction with Shiva was safe. Since then, he and I have collaborated on a number of projects, though I admit there have been times when, out of fear of what people might think, I haven't told others about his involvement.

In February 2021, I started working with another guide, Pietkela, who has declined to tell me what type of being he is, though he allows me to call him a being of light for the sake of convenience. As my guide, Pietkela has always been with me, but I didn't become aware of his presence until 2006, and I didn't realize he was actually my guide until February 2021. Pietkela now holds the role of my primary guide, which Shiva previously was, and in June 2021 took over providing me with the daily channeled messages.

I still work with Shiva as well as Pietkela. Both of them, having been with me for so long, have witnessed my experiences, their effects, and my healing journey. Both have given me support and encouragement as I've progressed. And both have messages they want to share with other people who have lived through experiences that have negatively impacted them.

I use the terms "trauma" and "trauma survivor" in my writing because they're what resonate for me, both for myself and in general, except when someone specifically asks me to use a different term for them. Because those are the terms I use, Shiva and Pietkela often use them as well since they recognize them as terms that have meaning for me and that I comprehend. If those terms don't work for you, as you read this book please mentally substitute whatever terms you prefer. As with almost all things in life, nothing is right for everyone. My guides are fond of saying "Words are just words and are for the benefit of humans who need to label things."

For that matter, some of Shiva's and Pietkela's messages as a whole may not resonate for you, or their way of phrasing things might not strike a chord. You're reading this book of your own free will, and your free will and intuition, along with any guidance you receive from your Core Self or your guides, is paramount over any words printed on these pages. Take what works and feels correct for you, and let the rest go.

I hope you'll take those last two paragraphs to heart. For myself, it's sometimes hard to set aside something an "expert" or "authority" says and listen to my own intuition and guidance instead. We survivors might have a hard time trusting ourselves because of past experiences or because people have told us we aren't to be trusted. As you read this book, I encourage you to exercise your powers of intuition, discernment, and free will. You don't have to agree with or listen to everything written here; you don't have to agree with or listen to any of it if none of it resonates for you. Let reading this book be an exercise for you in rebuilding trust in yourself.

Although my intention when I conceived of this project was to compile the daily channeled messages and then add new channeled material, Shiva and Pietkela had other ideas. Almost the entire book, aside from a few paragraphs here and there that I pulled from the daily messages, is new material. However, I'm including those daily messages at the end of the book for those who are interested in reading them.

Other than this introduction and my closing message at the end of the book, what you'll read comes from Shiva or Pietkela. They have chosen not to identify which of them contributed which piece other than their introductions, which follow this one.

It's our hope that the content of this book will bring you encouragement and compassion on your healing journey.

If you are in immediate crisis, in the United States dial 988 or text HOME to 741741. In Canada, dial 211. Other countries have resources as well; please reach out to find them or dial your country's emergency services number to get assistance.

Shiva's Introduction

For several lifetimes, I have worked with the being you know as River Lightbearer, whom I know as Ganatram. This being, this soul if that is a term which resonates for you, has experienced many things in their existence across multiple lifetimes.

Although the concept of "karma" is often misinterpreted, there is some truth to the idea that when one has caused harm in a lifetime, that harm may follow them into the next incarnation. Such has been the case for Ganatram. Although without malice, in previous lifetimes they brought harm to others, and in this they have chosen to learn to live without causing harm and to learn the pain they brought to others in previous lives.

This was a choice Ganatram made on a soul level between incarnations. It was not punishment, for there is no being, even the Ultimate Source, that would punish one for causing harm or making errors in their life. Punishment is not how one learns, either within an incarnate lifetime or across multiple lifetimes. Rather, Ganatram—or their soul—became aware of the harm caused and chose to make amends and to learn other ways of being.

This contributed to some of Ganatram's experiences in this lifetime. They occurred as part of lessons they chose to learn, or at the hands of reincarnated souls who had experienced harm from Ganatram in previous lifetimes.

I do not tell you this to state that any trauma you experience is because of a "soul contract" or "karma." Rather the opposite. The being Ganatram made this choice, but even so, much of what they have experienced in their current lifetime was not their choice and was outside of their control. Just as harm experienced at the hands of another is not punishment for past wrongs, neither is it a decision on the part of the one who receives that harm.

Many of you may have read or been told otherwise. You have been told that you were abused because of a "contract" between your soul and that of another, or that it is "karma" for damage you have caused others in previous lifetimes. You have been told that you "chose to learn lessons" through being abused or otherwise experiencing traumatic events. You have been told that you "magnetized" these events through your own energetic vibration and through not projecting "only positive vibes."

None of these things is true.

We—myself, the being referred to in this text as Pietkela, and other beings who work and interact with humans—wish to correct some of the misperceptions humans have developed about the workings of energy and reincarnation. We wish to eliminate the belief that any being is responsible for being harmed by another. And we wish to offer support and compassion to those of you who have been harmed by others, both overtly and through messages such as mentioned above.

No being deserves to be harmed. No being creates harm in their own life, for you can only create your actions and reactions. You do not create the choices and actions of others.

Some of the contents of this book may not resonate or ring true for you. Each sentient being is gifted with the power to discern what is and is not true for them, and it is our hope that you will read this text with that power in full effect. We do not purport to speak an ultimate truth, but simply the truth as we know it from our perspective, which is broader and closer to Source than the perspective humans have available.

At any time, you may choose to put down this book and leave it for a time. You may choose to set it aside permanently. You may even choose to fling it against a wall. All of these choices are valid. As you read, I encourage you to tend to your physical and emotional needs, for some aspects of this book may be upsetting or triggering for you. There is no shame in this. There is, however, a need to place your own well-being above anything else, including reading and gaining understanding through this text.

I am honored to contribute to this resource, and I hope that it will serve you.

Piethela's Introduction

J am not human. Therefore, the perspectives of humans are as alien to me as my perspectives may be to you. I am learning to comprehend the ways humans behave toward one another and the effects that behavior may have, and therefore my views upon the subjects of trauma and healing differ from views held by others, whether human or nonhuman.

However, one concept which exists throughout the Universe is that of responsibility. Each sentient being holds the power to be responsible for their own life. Each holds the power to create their own life. And each holds the power to discern positive, beneficial creations and choices from those which are negative or detrimental.

You have that power, but may have been unaware of it. You have created some aspects of your life, but not all, for you do not create what others choose to do or say. You are responsible for the choices you have made, but not for others' choices. At times the things you have done were not truly by choice, for they were caused by changes in your physiology or were done to protect yourself from others.

Responsibility and the power of creation are difficult concepts to put into human words, and they are deeper than can be discussed in the pages of a single book. Indeed, these concepts are ones which are debated and discussed throughout the Universe, and there is not always agreement upon what they truly mean or entail. I shall not endeavor to explain the concepts thoroughly here, but will simply state that they are understood in various ways, some of which are incorrect or are harmful to those of you who have experienced harm at the hands of others.

You are responsible for the conscious choices you make, but not all choices made by one who has experienced trauma are conscious. Some are made on a deeper level, in a part of the brain that is not subject to conscious thought or control. This part has been altered by the traumatic experiences until it no longer is able to react to reality, but rather acts out of the mistaken belief that harm is still occurring and will continue and always occur. This belief is not a choice, as it is not conscious; the autonomic system of the brain and nerves are what cause it, and it cannot be addressed or changed simply by wishing to do so.

Even when you are not responsible for the actions and speech caused by this autonomic portion of your physiology, you are responsible for the repercussions. You may not be consciously aware of causing problems for another, or may not realize that you are speaking in a harsh tone or are rejecting one who wishes to aid you. However, if this is brought to your awareness along with the impact those actions have caused, you are responsible for recognizing that you have caused pain or harm and for making apologies or amends. It is truth to say, "I was unaware." It is not truth to say, "I'm not responsible because I was traumatized."

You are not responsible for what others have visited upon you. On no level did you "choose a lesson to be learned" through being harmed. On no level did you agree to experiencing harm at the hands of another. This is a fallacy often stated by those who either wish to blame people for being recipients of harm or by those who wish to believe they had control over their own abuse and harm. If believing this about yourself brings you peace and understanding, I will not dissuade you from it; however, I caution you against attempting to force others to believe they are at fault—on any level, whether before or during this incarnation—for harm done to them.

I have contributed to this book both as an individual and speaking for the Collaboration, a collective of which I am part. I will not differentiate between the two, for even when speaking for my collective, I use my own words. Know, however, that as you read this book, the guidance and information you receive comes from many sources, and it is our hope that all of it will benefit you.

You have never been at fault for what occurred in your past. You have never given cause for any other to treat you poorly or harm you. You deserve to progress and find support on your healing journey, and if this book has found its way to you, you are ready to begin or progress further upon that journey.

We hope to aid you as you progress and grow, and we hope to assure you that nothing in your life has altered your core Self, even though it has altered certain facets of your physiology and personality. That Self lies deeper than can be touched by trauma or any other experience, and so is there, waiting until you are able to reconnect with and live as it.

You deserve to be whole, though you have never truly been broken.

You Did Not Choose This

*J*n life, humans have many experiences. Some of these are positive and beneficial. Some are not.

Each experience leaves its imprint upon you. Each incident and event you undergo will have an effect. These effects are not solely within your mind.

When an experience is harmful, the impact left behind can alter the very way in which you live. Your entire being, physical, mental, emotional, and energetic, is changed by what has occurred. This is not something you choose to have happen, but rather is the result of undergoing harmful experiences.

What humans call "trauma" is not the incident or your thoughts about it, but rather the total of all effects caused by what has occurred. Trauma is the impact, not the event. If trauma is present, it means that your physiology has been altered. Your brain responds to threats that do not exist in the current moment, or perceives current threat even if none is present. Your autonomic system reacts in a way intended to defend or protect you from these threats. Since this system does not recognize the passage of time, these reactions are the same as that which you may have experienced at the time of the actual event.

On an emotional level, you may find yourself feeling things that are not relevant to a current situation or are out of proportion to what is currently happening. This is because your current emotions are fueled by your past experiences, particularly if you were unable or forbidden to express how you felt about the incident when it occurred. When you have been forced to suppress your emotions out of fear or out of a belief that you somehow do not deserve to express yourself, it becomes difficult to feel and express emotions appropriately.

At times, your mind may recreate the harmful experience in such detail that you are unable to distinguish the mind's creation from your current reality. This is what humans term a "flashback." Flashbacks are not simply memories of harmful events, but are rather full-immersion experiences. All aspects of you react as if what your mind is creating is a current reality. These creations are not intentional on your part, but rather are the remnants of your past that have become stuck or imprinted upon your mind.

When you experience a flashback, your actions and words may be appropriate to what your mind has created but not to the actual circumstance in the present moment. This, too, is not your choice. It is not your "fault" when you react to a flashback as if it were a true occurrence. These reactions and responses are also part of the changes that were caused in your brain and mind when the events occurred.

There is no fault. There is no blame. We encourage you to refrain from blaming yourself when you react in a way that is not accurate or proportionate for your current circumstances. We likewise encourage you to refrain from blaming those who harmed you. While the harm was indeed their responsibility, holding them at fault only causes you to dwell deep within your anger, and this will impede your healing.

You are not called upon to "forgive" those who have harmed you, nor to "let go" of your anger or the other effects of your experiences. Indeed, letting go of some of those effects would be impossible as they are now hard-wired, so to speak, in your physiology, your mind, and your energy system. You can no more "just let go" of these effects than you could simply let go of a physical wound or illness.

We will speak more about forgiveness and responsibility in later chapters. Our intention in this beginning is to inform you of what trauma means, what it is, and what it does. Although you are one who is living with trauma and therefore may have knowledge and understanding, often survivors are hardest upon themselves and other survivors because they don't understand the truth of trauma or because they wish the truth to be different.

River has stated that they have received greater condemnation from other survivors than from those who have not experienced trauma when they have stated that one cannot "get over" trauma solely by wishing it or that it is not a survivor's choice to be impacted by their experiences. We have seen also, with River and with others we have observed, that survivors tend to condemn themselves and even veer toward self-hatred for things which are outside of their choice or control.

We wish to change these perceptions. We wish those who read these words to recognize and understand that trauma is not simply "choosing to feel bad about the past," as some have phrased it. It is, rather, an autonomic and automatic response to harmful or painful events. One does not choose to be traumatized, just as one does not choose to be wounded when cut with a knife. One does not choose to experience physical and mental effects of trauma, just as one does not choose to cough and sneeze when infected by a cold virus.

At its most basic, trauma is the collection of detrimental physical, mental/emotional, and energetic effects and changes left behind by an experience. These effects include alterations in the various nervous systems of the body, which may lead to such occurrences as fighting, fleeing, or freezing in the face of an incident which others may find benign. The effects include changes in bodily functions such as digestion and elimination. They include changes in the levels and release processes of certain hormones, which can in turn lead to physical health issues such as autoimmune disorders.

Trauma is far from simple, and it is far more than simply being "stuck in the past," as some term it, or having unpleasant memories of an experience. Human science, including medicine and psychiatry, are still learning all of the aspects and impacts of trauma. For this reason, trauma is still often misunderstood and misidentified as "laziness," as a refusal to "move on" or "get over it," and as something to be stigmatized and even bullied out of people rather than something to accept and view with compassion.

It is our hope that through reading this book, you will learn to view yourself and others with compassion when trauma symptoms arise. We seek to aid and empower those who have experienced trauma to recognize the far reaches of the effects and impacts, and to help you gain a voice and the words to use to explain this to others.

River is not a professional, but is one who has studied trauma and its effects, primarily in an effort to understand and accept themself more fully. We who are contributing our knowledge and words to this project are likewise not professionals; as River has phrased it, few institutions are willing to convey degrees and certifications upon disembodied beings. The understanding and definitions of trauma and its effects come equally from River's studies and from our perspectives as beings of higher vibration and broader knowledge. We encourage you to read with discernment, for what we say may not resonate for you or you may have been taught differently, and we do not seek to assert ourselves as ultimate authorities on this subject.

Indeed, for some who have experienced traumatic events, authority is a difficult concept, for the abuse and harm you experienced may have come at the hands of those who claimed authority over you. This has caused you to become distrustful of those who state or imply authority. This fear and distrust is understandable but is something which holds you back in some ways, so you are encouraged to address it when you are able.

Because trauma impacts mind, physiology, and energy, the effects are broad and deep. Some are unaware that some of the issues they experience are directly due to past traumatic events. Unfortunately, even some professionals are unaware that a person's resistance to certain treatments or need for minute details of a process might be due to trauma, and those professionals may become frustrated or even state that the person does not wish to receive treatment or improve.

You are not in control of the effects traumatic events have upon your mind, body, and energy. You do not choose to have your nervous, mental, and energy systems altered to the extent that you respond to current circumstances as if they are the same as the trauma of the past. You do not choose to have holes and blocks in your chakras and energy field. You do not choose to distrust others or to require reassurance and details in order to form some semblance of trust.

You do not choose to feel, at times, as if the traumatic events of the past are occurring in the present moment. This is another function of your subconscious and your autonomic systems. Certain stimuli trigger a response in you that was formed during the time of trauma. Because the systems involved in these responses are deeper than your consciousness, they do not recognize or comprehend the passage of time. To those systems, everything is "now." Everything occurs in the present moment, regardless of chronological time.

Therefore, those systems create reactions that were appropriate or necessary during the original events, and may even cause you to experience sensory input such as sights and sounds that were present during those events but do not exist in your present external reality. This is what is termed a "flashback," and the stimuli and associated responses are what is meant by "being triggered." A trigger does not remind you of the event and is not something which merely upsets you; it is something which causes you to become fully immersed in the re-experiencing of past events.

You did not choose the events which occurred in the past, nor did you choose the impacts of those events upon you. You do not choose to be triggered by certain stimuli. This is the primary point we wish you to internalize. You did not choose this. You did not create it. You were not subject to those experiences due to "low vibration" or "negative thoughts." If you have been told these things, know that they are false.

However, you have the power to choose whether and how to manage and mitigate the effects. Within you, you carry the ability to learn to navigate the world while honoring and working with the changes that have been made to your systems. You do not choose the effects, but you can learn to choose how you react and respond to current circumstances, even those which put you in a state of feeling as if the trauma is still occurring.

Just as external intervention may be necessary in healing physical injuries and illness, so it might be beneficial in progressing in healing trauma. We do not use the term "healing" lightly when we speak of trauma, for in truth there is no such thing as "fully healed," though some will state otherwise. We shall speak more of the healing journey and how one might progress in a later chapter.

For now, we shall leave it that healing is indeed a journey, one which lasts a lifetime and perhaps into future lives. You will heal some aspects of the trauma, some aspects of yourself, only to find deeper wounds that then require healing. This does not mean you are irreparably damaged. Far from it. Rather, it means that the wounds and effects designated by the term "trauma" are more complex and run deeper than humans may realize, and because of this, the process of healing will be longer and may include complications and regressions.

Therefore, when we speak of healing, we speak of the process and progression rather than something with a finite end. In this process you may, at times, benefit from external assistance. No human exists in full isolation, though at times many of you feel otherwise. Each of you has access to other humans who will aid you if asked, whether because they are paid to do so as in the case of professionals, or because they care for you and wish to see you improve as in the case of friends and loved ones.

Trusting these people to assist you, regardless of whether they are professionals or have a more personal connection to you, may be difficult. You have, after all, been taught that people are not to be trusted. Your experiences may have impressed upon you the idea that trusting someone will lead to harm and pain. Even if you have consciously reached an awareness that this is not always the case, your deeper mind, the aspects of you most affected by your experiences, may not believe that trust is possible.

You also may have learned, either through experience or by being explicitly told, that you must rely only upon yourself. That seeking aid is weakness, and that no one would wish to help you anyway. Again, these are beliefs that you may now be able to refute with your conscious mind, but the deeper mind still holds them.

Because the effects of trauma run deep and impact many systems and aspects of your body, mind, energy, and indeed your very self, it is highly advisable to seek aid in addressing them. Not only advisable, but also beneficial, for by seeking and receiving aid and compassion from other humans, you will begin to counteract some of the trauma effects. This is not a journey you must undertake alone. It is one for which you deserve and are encouraged to seek support.

You did not choose to experience events which led to trauma. You did not choose the harmful actions and words of others. Nor did you choose the impacts and effects those events left upon you. But you are able, now, to choose whether to address those impacts and effects. You are able to decide whether you wish to continue living in a state in which your every thought and action are impacted by the past, or whether you wish to learn strategies and mechanisms for managing the responses and reactions created by your autonomic systems.

It is common for those who have experienced traumatic events to state such things as "my power was stolen" or "I need to take back my power." These sentiments are understandable but inaccurate. Your power is an intrinsic part of you. It cannot be stolen from you, for it comes from the Core Self within you that has existed since long before your current incarnation. Your power was never taken away; it was suppressed and hidden from you, perhaps for your own protection, perhaps because those who harmed you persuaded you that it did not exist. But it has remained within you nonetheless.

As your power was never stolen or taken away, there is no need to "take it back." Instead, the call you hear now is to uncover your power. To bring it out of hiding and learn once again to utilize it for your benefit, both in general and in the healing journey you have chosen to undertake.

Some of you may be frightened at the prospect of being powerful, and this, too, is understandable. However, the power within you is part of the Self which knows how to wield this power without harm or force. You have learned to distrust yourself as well as others; therefore, one of your first steps is to regain enough trust in yourself to realize that your inner power is not something you will abuse, but rather something you may learn to embrace.

This power will benefit you in a number of ways. You will learn that you are able to choose the course of your life. You will gain the discernment to enable you to choose wisely. Most importantly, you will learn that you need not listen to what others tell you, for they do not know you as well as you know yourself. They can only observe and state their thoughts. They cannot truly know what is best for you or what thoughts and ideas are in your mind.

Nor can they know the full extent of the effects your experiences have had upon you, for even you cannot know this. Others may believe they know what trauma does. They may believe, based upon what they have seen of you, that they know what it has done to you specifically. But they do not truly know what changes have occurred within your systems, nor the underlying reasons and motivations for your actions and words. As you may not be fully aware of these yourself, it is impossible that another could know. No one knows you better than you, even if they claim or pretend otherwise.

Embracing your inner power will enable you to release the fears and anxieties about what others may think of you. It will help you to realize that you are autonomous and owe no one explanations or justifications for your choices, particularly when those choices are healthy and of benefit to you. Autonomy does not mean you may do whatever you wish; this is another common misconception held by some humans. It means, rather, that you have the power to make your own decisions and follow your own course without being required to have approval or permission from others.

If your choices cause pain or harm to others, if exercising your own power and autonomy infringes upon others' ability to exercise theirs, it is your responsibility to acknowledge what you have done and apologize or make amends where possible. Part of being autonomous is learning to take responsibility for your actions and words. Your autonomy does not extend to interference with others' right or ability to live their lives in safe and healthy ways.

Indeed, choice and freedom are concepts with which humans struggle, for some define them in ways that include interference with others. We shall discuss this more in a later chapter, for understanding the bounds and limits of your freedom is a vital part of healing. You cannot progress in your own healing journey when you are knowingly and intentionally inflicting harm upon others from which they will need to heal.

Others may use their power to attempt to control you or manage your healing. They may believe their autonomy, or "sovereignty" as some term it, permits them to cause you further harm or negate your feelings and thoughts about their behavior. They are not acting in a correct manner, for enforcing one's power upon another is never correct. Believing that one's autonomy overrules everyone else's is never correct.

These people may be acting out of the results of their own

harmful experiences or may be operating under misunderstandings gained from incorrect teachings. The reason does not matter and is stated only to encourage you to feel compassion for these people if you are willing, for many of them do not act out of malice. They simply are unable to recognize the harm they are causing because they have not been taught to live their lives in nonharmful ways, though they may believe otherwise.

Choosing to connect with and accept your own inner power will shield you from the impact of those who exercise theirs incorrectly. When you claim your power and use it to guide your life and manage your reactions to external stimuli, those who attempt to force power over you or who compromise your rights and freedoms in the name of asserting their own will be unable to affect you. You may, in fact, become one who speaks out against that behavior and teaches the correct ways to embrace and utilize one's inner power.

You did not choose the events of your past, nor the lasting effects those events have left behind in your body, mind, and energy. However, you now have the power to choose how and whether to heal from those events. You may now choose the next stage of your life journey and how best to progress in it. Many choices are open to you when you are able to understand that you did not choose to be harmed and therefore do not deserve continued suffering because of the actions of others.

Those actions were *their* choices, not yours. It is now time to make your own choices.

There Js No Fault, There Js No Blame

*T*he only path or process in a healing journey that is not valid is one which results in harm to you or another. Causing harm, particularly when it is done with knowledge and intention, is never a valid option, for this renders you little better than those who deliberately harmed you.

If accidental harm is caused by a process you have chosen, it is wisest to acknowledge the harm, apologize if the harm was to another, and make amends where it is possible. Even in the midst of your healing journey, even as you process your own pain and the harm done to you, there is no justification for harming another. You are responsible for your actions and the results thereof.

However, being responsible does not equate to being at fault, and does not require blaming yourself for what you have done.

Taking this responsibility, accepting and honoring it, is a step in the healing journey. When one has been harmed by others, it becomes second nature to blame the experiences, and therefore those who inflicted the harm, for one's struggles and shortcomings. Although your way of navigating the world has unquestionably been affected by what has occurred, still it is your responsibility to be aware of how your actions and words may affect others. It is your responsibility to learn other ways of navigating the world so that minimal, if any, harm is caused.

Accepting this responsibility can be a difficult step for some, for you have been told that you are responsible for what was done to you. Some of you, in fact, have been told that nothing was "done to you," but rather that you chose the occurrences. These statements are false, though they do not come from a deliberate intention of falsehood. These beliefs are due to misperceptions and misunderstandings of some universal truths.

You are encouraged to remember that people who have stated these things to you may be operating out of their own misconceptions. Some of them may even take comfort in the idea that they caused or created the abuse they experienced. It is not for you to attempt to correct how they view the world; however, it is equally unnecessary for you to accept what they have told you.

Your responsibility begins and ends with your own actions, thoughts, and words. You bear no responsibility for what others choose to do or say. This does not mean that you are not responsible if your actions or words harm another, however, although some humans say differently. As you are responsible for your choices, you are also responsible for the impact those choices have upon others. This is why it is necessary in your healing journey that you learn to accept your responsibilities and to make apologies or amends where possible to those who have been harmed, however unintentionally on your part, by things you have said or done.

When your words or actions harm another, this is indeed your responsibility, for you have caused the harm. They are not responsible for being harmed, just as you are not responsible for harm others have caused to you. Because of your experiences, you may not know alternative ways of interacting with others or of responding to intense emotions, but this does not absolve you of responsibility for what you do or say or for the repercussions of those choices.

As you progress in your healing journey, you will learn to identify the choices you make which are problematic for you and others. You will learn to recognize alternate choices and to make the choices which cause the least harm to the fewest people. At times, your choices may still cause harm, but this will become an unintentional effect. However, no matter how unintentional the harm, you still have the responsibility to apologize and make amends where possible, for you are responsible for what occurs even if it is not what you intended.

At times, you will feel guilt when you realize you have harmed others. This guilt may extend to events in the past when someone else was harmed by your choices. We encourage you to work toward releasing this, for guilt is not a productive emotion. Feeling guilt does not resolve issues nor make amends for harm. It only provides something in which to wallow and stagnate. You cannot make progress when you cling to guilt or allow it to rule your thoughts and self-perception, for it will cause you to remain in one place, as it were. You need not feel guilt in order to recognize and accept your responsibility. Indeed, it will impede you from making amends with those you have harmed.

Although you are ultimately responsible for the choices you make, we encourage you to remember that when you choose harmful actions, it may be due to not knowing the alternatives. Some of these choices you have made came about because it was what you had learned and observed, and you knew no other course of action or were unable to consider another course because your emotions were heightened or you were triggered into responding as if trauma was occurring at that moment. These explanations, these reasons, also do not absolve you of responsibility, but they do provide a reason for compassion. You can learn other ways of behaving, but when you know no other way, your choices may be viewed with compassion while still affirming their inappropriateness.

In your life, you have been told, perhaps repeatedly, that you are a "bad person." You have been told that you are responsible for others' abuse of you because of who you are or imagined actions you have committed. Even if you were not told these things overtly, they were likely part and parcel of the abuse and harm you experienced, for those who consciously choose to inflict harm do not accept responsibility for their actions. They prefer to place blame upon their targets rather than acknowledging that they themselves made the choice to cause harm.

Particularly if your experiences occurred when you were a child, you likely created your own narrative of fault and blame. Those inflicting harm upon you may have appeared to others to be "good people." You may even have attempted to report what was occurring and been accused of lying or making it up based upon how the one harming you behaved toward others. If the one causing harm was your parent or caregiver, this denial and negation of you ran deeper still, for a child believes themself responsible for everything that occurs to and around them, and humans are taught that their parents are supposed to love and protect them. When a parent behaves contrary to this belief, the child comes to blame themself, for they think they must be a horrible child in order for their parents to choose not to act in the manner you are taught parents will act.

This belief, this self-blame, furthers your guilt when another is harmed by your actions or words, indirectly. You may even blame yourself if someone for whom you care is harmed by something done by another, for you absorb the guilt which may be unfelt by the one causing the harm.

However, self-blame does not ameliorate pain. It does not change the situation. And often, it is unnecessary and harmful to you.

We encourage you to recognize the bounds and limits of your responsibility and to reconsider the concepts of "blame" and "fault." These concepts are unwarranted, for there is no fault or blame. Blaming another confers upon them a power they do not truly possess. Likewise, blaming yourself implies that you have power over things which are not actually within your purview. Similarly, accepting fault or feeling guilt implies that your power and responsibility extend beyond their true limits.

A more beneficial view is to consider responsibility rather than fault. You are responsible for your choices and actions and for the consequences thereof. Others are responsible for their choices and actions and for those consequences. When your choices cause harm to another, you are responsible for that harm because it is a direct result of your choice. When another harms you, they are responsible for that harm.

Holding another responsible for their actions and the results of those actions is acceptable. Holding yourself responsible for what you do and say is likewise acceptable. However, holding yourself or another responsible is not the same as blaming them. Assigning responsibility is largely a function of rational thought. It is, for the most part, objective. However, assigning fault or blame is a function of emotions. It often carries guilt, anger, and even hatred. It is subjective and can become destructive.

You are asked to remember that you are not responsible for what others do or say, but you are responsible for any actions or words on your part that spur their actions. To provide a clearer example, if your friend yells at you and calls you names, that is their responsibility. It is their choice. However, if they are doing so because they feel anger toward you for insulting them behind their back, you are responsible for having insulted them and therefore have a responsibility to apologize or make amends to them.

You may, of course, also choose not to do this, knowing that it may result in the end of the friendship, something for which you would be partially responsible as it is a result of your choices. Your friend would also bear some responsibility for the friendship ending, for it would also be a result of their choices. In some interactions and situations, each person involved bears some responsibility.

However, that is not the case for abuse and other inflictions of harm. The recipient of harm or abuse holds no responsibility for it. Abuse is not an interaction between two people in the same way as an argument or other conflict. It is, rather, an enforcement of one's power over another. The one enforcing the power is the only one responsible, regardless of their proclaimed reason for doing so. There is no action one can commit that justifies abuse from another.

The concepts of responsibility, fault, and blame are ones often misunderstood, sometimes willfully. These words, as with many in certain human languages, are open to interpretation and have different meanings to various people. There is no single correct way to view the concepts; there are, however, incorrect ways, including those ways which force guilt upon others or attempt to hold people responsible for actions committed by others.

As you progress in your healing journey, be mindful of how you act toward others. It is not uncommon for one who has experienced trauma to unwittingly inflict harm upon others because of unawareness of how their actions affect people or because of lack of understanding of other ways to conduct their lives. While it is virtually impossible to live a life without at times causing pain or even harm, it is possible to become increasingly cognizant of your actions and how they impact those around you. And it is possible to learn less harmful ways of interacting.

You are not responsible for others' actions or words, but you are responsible for the effects of your actions and words. If you are told you have harmed or hurt someone through something you have said or done, it is your responsibility. In these instances, you are encouraged to acknowledge what you have done and validate how they feel, for all feelings are valid and it is not for you to deny hurting someone who says you have caused them pain. You yourself have been invalidated by those who harmed you. Refrain from doing this to others.

Refrain, in fact, from doing this to yourself, for it is often the case that one who has experienced harm and invalidation turns to harming and invalidating themself. This is not necessarily a choice made on a conscious level but rather is another example of not knowing a different way to behave or being unaware of the effect you are having. You may have internalized what was said or done to you and the impressions left by those things. Even if the people who harmed you are no longer present in your life, their voices still are, living within your mind and speaking as if separate entities.

These voices, which are in reality variations of your own voice, will convince you that those who harmed you were right. They will persuade you that you and you alone are at fault for what was done. They will state repeatedly that you are a "bad person" who deserves harm and detriment.

These voices are not real. They are aspects of you, pieces splintered and damaged by the experiences of your past. They do not speak truth, for they do not truly exist. They are part of you but are also echoes of voices long gone from your life, or of voices still present but less vocal than in the past.

We invite you to consider the things these voices tell you, for what is said comes from within your own mind, even if it was planted there by others. It comes from your ego, that part of you which simultaneously wishes to be superior and believes itself to be inferior. It comes from what some humans call their "shadows" or their "inner children," pieces of themselves frozen at times of trauma which constantly relive those experiences until the conscious self learns to work in collaboration with them to heal and form a more beneficial life.

However, in many cases, the words spoken by these inner voices do not originate in your own mind but in the minds and mouths of those who caused you harm. The deeper reaches of your mind recorded these statements, particularly those you heard over and over, and held them until you were no longer able to consciously recognize their origins and instead believed them to be your own truths and perceptions.

These voices are often where guilt and shame have their genesis, for the people who implanted these ideas often expected you to accept blame and be ashamed of what they were doing to you so they would not have to accept responsibility. You have learned and internalized the concept that you are at fault for every detrimental thing that occurs. You have learned to be ashamed not only of the things you do but of things others have done to you.

Guilt and shame are human emotions like many others, but they have no place in a beneficial life. They serve no purpose, and they do not change the past or present and will not aid you in creating a more pleasant future. We will not tell you how you should feel nor command you to release any emotion, for this is not our role and all emotions are valid. However, we will encourage you to work toward eliminating guilt and shame from your range of emotions, for of all emotions experienced by humans, these are among the most harmful.

You need feel no shame for what has occurred in your life. Some of it was outside your control, and as you are not responsible, you need not feel shame. Even the occurrences for which you do bear responsibility are nothing for which shame is warranted. You may have done or experienced things you now wish had not occurred, and that is valid, but this does not mean shame is necessary. The experiences cannot be erased; they have occurred. You may choose how you think and feel about them. Even things you now wish you had not done, presuming those things were within your control at all, are things from which perhaps you learned or gained some benefit.

Likewise with guilt. There is no need for it, nor does it bring any purpose or benefit. Actions you committed voluntarily may have caused harm, and for this you may feel sadness or anger toward yourself, but these emotions are not the same as guilt. Sadness and anger are emotions which may, in some way, become productive. Guilt is only destructive. Accept the things you have done and the pain or harm you caused, make amends and apologies where you are able, and attempt to replace your guilt with more useful emotions.

There is no fault. There is no blame. You did not cause others to harm you. You have not chosen the effects and results of that harm. You did choose actions and words that may have harmed others, but you did not do so with the intention of bringing harm, and you may now learn from those experiences and endeavor to make amends to those who were harmed as well as knowing more beneficial ways of interacting and navigating your life in the future.

Again, there is no fault. There is no blame. We encourage you to cease turning these things upon yourself and others. There is only responsibility, and we encourage you to learn the bounds and limits of yours.

More Than a Sum

You are more than the sum of your parts.

To some of you, this phrase sounds cliched. It is something you have heard many times in many contexts, and it has ceased to have meaning for you.

In this context, however, it has a very specific meaning. You are more than the sum of your experiences. You are far greater and more powerful than anything that has occurred in your life, whether positive or negative.

In your life, you have had negative experiences. Some of these have resulted in trauma, in the alteration of physiology and biology into something that causes specific reactions and behaviors as well as physical and mental symptoms. As stated previously, the meaning of trauma is not the experiences themselves, but rather the results thereof. When your brain, mind, body, and energy are altered negatively by an experience, this is trauma.

But even these alterations do not comprise who you are, for you are not the body or energy field in which you dwell. These things are temporary. They are the constructs created for the lifetime you are currently living. Even when they have been changed, your Core Self, the "you" whom you have been from the moment of your creation, is not affected.

This Self is what some may call a soul, and yet it is more than that, for it is the very essence of your being. It is the part of you that knows, that hears, that loves. It is the part that grows and learns.

It is the part that cannot be touched by anything that occurs within a given lifetime, even when the occurrences are traumatic.

This does not mean you have been unaffected by your experiences. Those events have had effects and impacts on you, some lasting longer than others. Some of these impacts may last throughout this lifetime and even be carried into others, for your energy at times carries over into future lifetimes and this energy carries the imprint of all experiences. On a shallower level, everything you experience in your life, no matter how seemingly small or large, no matter how positive or negative, does cause effects.

These effects, however, do not comprise who you truly are. They are things beyond your conscious control, as they have been caused by the alteration of your functioning in this human body. They are things which at times impede your ability to function and lead a positive and beneficial life. We do not seek to minimize or ignore the impacts of traumatic events on any human, for many of you have been so impacted, and too many of you have had your experiences brushed off or invalidated. That is not our purpose.

It is necessary for some of you to fully understand the truth that trauma is not the experiences you have had. It is the effects of those experiences upon your mind, body, and energy. Therefore, stating that an experience was not traumatic, or being invalidated by another because the experience wasn't "bad enough" to traumatize, is inaccurate. Any experience which causes the long-term effects on your mind, body, and energy is traumatic. If these effects occur, the experience was indeed "bad enough."

However, each of you is an individual, and the reactions to and effects of experiences, even should those experiences be similar or identical, will vary from one person to another. This is a reason why judging your experiences by comparing to those of others does not serve you. Their experience may seem "worse" than yours. They may have sustained more severe immediate effects such as physical injuries. But that is not the measure of trauma. The long-term effects and the alterations caused by what occurred are what comprise the condition known as trauma, and having these reactions, alterations, and effects is valid regardless of how seemingly severe or minor the incident or sequence of events was.

You do not choose trauma. The changes which occur in your mind, body, and energy are the result of both external and internal factors, but none of those factors is a conscious choice on your part. The physiological systems involved when a potentially traumatizing event occurs are autonomic or involuntary; these reactions, such as what humans term "fight, flight, or freeze," occur without conscious thought or decision. The system senses a threat and takes action to protect the being as a whole. It is no more a conscious choice than requiring oxygen.

Some of you condemn yourselves for your reactions to traumatic events and for how you subsequently navigate the world. You view yourselves as broken or damaged because you are unable to function as you believe a "normal" person would. You look down upon yourself and think or speak of yourself harshly because you are unable to change your reactions and behaviors, or are able to do so only with a great deal of effort.

You are not broken, beloveds. None of you has ever been broken, for your Core Self, the untouched essence of who you are, remains intact no matter what occurs. It is true that damage has been done to you, but this damage is reparable. What has been altered may, with effort, be re-altered, or you may learn new pathways, new patterns, which will serve you without impact from the trauma.

In the meantime, your reactions and your way of functioning and navigating in the world are not your choice and are far from a sign of weakness or flaw. They are, indeed, signs of strength, for without inner strength you would not have survived the events or would have given up on caring about the effects. The very fact that you are aware that some patterns and behaviors are detrimental to you or others demonstrates your strength, and this strength is what has brought you to your current point.

Your strength was not forged in fire, as some may say. You are not strong because of your experiences, but rather completely separate from them. That strength has always dwelled within you, and it would have been present regardless of whether your life ran smoothly or as it did. Some humans will, of course, say otherwise; human beliefs and understanding vary. However, we assert that your strength belongs to you and was innate within you long before any of your life experiences.

Because of this, there is no need to "be grateful" for your experiences. There is no need to feel or express gratitude for that which has harmed you or to the people who caused that harm. This, too, is something about which beliefs differ. Should you feel drawn to express and feel gratitude for having had traumatizing experiences, this is a choice you are free to make, for even in differences of beliefs, free will exists. For some of you, being grateful for your experiences and to those who caused those experiences brings you peace. As this book is intended to bring further peace to you, we do not speak against any belief or activity which creates peace for you.

However, for some of you, being commanded to feel and express gratitude for harmful experiences and to abusive people has caused you further harm. You have found yourselves unable to feel gratitude for the pain and damage which was conferred upon you. You have cut ties with those who harmed you or have limited your exposure to them, and they or others have told you this is wrong and you must forgive.

There is no "must" as you progress in your healing journey. There is no requirement to forgive or be grateful. Whatever choice brings you peace and helps you progress is the correct choice to make, even if others tell you that you are wrong. They are not on your journey. Only you are on your path; only you can determine how best to proceed.

Additionally, only you have a full understanding of what you have experienced and what effects it has wrought upon you. Others may attempt to tell you that you are wrong, that trauma "does not work that way," or that the things you have undergone are not traumatic. This is not their decision to make, for they are not you and have not had your experiences. Nor do they dwell within your mind, subject to the changes the trauma has caused.

Humankind is still learning the vast reaches and structures of what you call your mind. Some use this term synonymously with "brain," yet they are not the same. Your brain is solely the physical organ residing within your skull. Your mind is all the things of which that organ is capable, all the perceptions and senses which are yet to be recognized by human science, all the places and dimensions to which you travel in physical reality and in dreams and visions.

When we state that your mind is altered, we refer both to the physical organ, the brain, and to those perceptions and senses. Trauma impacts all of it.

Because human science and medicine do not yet fully understand the brain and mind, they cannot fully understand trauma and its effects. And if scientists and doctors do not possess this understanding, it is unreasonable to expect a layperson to possess it.

Many of the statements which bring further harm to those who have experienced trauma come from this lack of understanding rather than from any malicious intent or desire to negate another. This does not minimize the harm these statements cause, but it is our hope that if you have received these statements, you will be able to see that they are untrue not because the speaker is lying or attempting to hurt you, but because they, as a human being, cannot yet fully understand the effects of your experiences or of their words.

Even those of us who exist in higher dimensions, who are able to perceive and access a broader array of knowledge and information, do not fully comprehend the human brain nor the human propensity toward inflicting harm upon one another. Gaining this comprehension and aiding humans in changing the tendency toward harm are among the reasons we choose to work with you.

We do not claim we can alter the entire course of human behavior, nor would we wish to do so even if we had that ability. However, we wish to connect with those of you who understand and experience love and compassion, for you are those who will assist your world in reaching a point where less harm is caused and more people are able to accept and support one another.

You are in the world for a purpose, but receiving harm is not part of that purpose. You were not birthed into your current form in your current time to learn or teach lessons that involve pain or damage, for this is not how the Creator seeks to teach. Lessons may be chosen by each individual prior to or even during existence, but those lessons do not necessitate being the recipient of abuse or trauma, despite what some humans state to the contrary. Neither you nor those who have inflicted harm upon you are learning any lesson by doing so, and you are not in the world to receive harm so that another may learn not to cause it.

Rather, your purpose is to create a life in which you are able to give and receive love. A life in which change occurs subject to your will and your choices. A life in which you are, for want of a better term, happy. You may, on a discarnate level, have chosen subjects about which you wished to learn in this current lifetime. Those subjects and lessons may, as some humans state, have been chosen based upon experiences in previous incarnations. However, while your purpose does include learning and growth, it does not include pain and harm. Those are chosen by the ones who inflict it, not on a "soul level" by the recipient.

We understand that for some of you, hearing that you do not choose or create the harm that is done to you is as painful as hearing that it is a choice is to others. We do not wish to cause you pain or cognitive dissonance by stating that you are not responsible for the creation of harm or its repercussions in your life. If you feel pain or anger at these words as you read, if what is printed upon the page feels wrong or dissonant to you, you may of course choose to reject it and believe what brings you peace. We simply encourage you, in that instance, to recognize that it is not for you to force your beliefs upon others or blame them for their experiences if you choose to blame yourself for yours.

For those others who have heard those words and been harmed by them, or who have rejected those words out of a sense of falsehood, know that they are indeed untrue. No being chooses to be harmed. Not in their current existence and not in any existence between lifetimes. You did not choose what occurred.

Nor did you create it through any negative beliefs or low-vibration thinking. While it is true to some extent that you attract people and circumstances which are a match or close to your own vibration, you do not create harm that occurs in your life. You do not bring this to you through your vibration even if your vibration is low.

When your energetic vibration is lowered, others with low vibration may be drawn to you, and these may be the people who bring you harm. However, you did not create the harm and you did not choose to bring those people into your life. Energetic resonance is not a conscious choice; while your vibration is subject to choice to some extent, you must first be aware that you have the choice to make and then be aware of what your vibration is. This is not something with which many humans are familiar, and therefore we cannot say that humans choose to have low vibrations or to attract others with similar vibrations.

Harm is the choice, the creation, and the responsibility of the one inflicting the harm. That is the whole of the truth.

Because you did not create the harm that was done and did not choose it, your true Self remains unchanged, though not unaffected, by it. When you receive a physical injury such as a cut or broken bone, you would not say that this injury has changed who you are on a fundamental level. The same is true for the injury of trauma. It changes your reactions and responses to certain stimuli and may alter how you view the world and yourself, but it does not and cannot change who you are at your core.

That Core Self is so much more than we can put into words. It is the sum of every lifetime you have lived, every moment spent between lifetimes, every experience you have had. It is the knowledge and wisdom carried from the Universe itself. It is a being of light and joy, and although it lives within a physical form, it is not altered by what the form experiences. It is affected in that this Self shares the emotions of the conscious self, and the Core Self sorrows at the conscious self's pain, but it is not changed.

Indeed, the Self reflects the Universe as a whole, for the Universe itself sorrows when any of its parts hurts. When any of its parts is harmed by another. The Universe, or perhaps you prefer to call it the Creator or God or another term, wishes each being to be well, to be loved and at peace, though it cannot intervene to force this state into being. Therefore, when one experiences unwellness, poor treatment, hatred, the Universe mourns what might have been.

However, the Universe does not condemn. It does not judge. It merely is saddened when one of its parts harms another. Sadness and sorrow are not judgment.

Although it is human nature to condemn and judge one another, we ask that you work toward releasing this tendency, particularly as it applies to yourself. Many humans judge others, but those who have experienced trauma often judge themselves more harshly than they would even consider judging another person. This judgment toward yourself does not serve you, for it only furthers the harm that has been done. You may be away from the person who inflicted the harm, but when you judge yourself and condemn your own actions and choices, you are taking the role of that person.

You are not deserving of judgment and condemnation. Even if you have inflicted harm upon others yourself, still you do not deserve to be judged or condemned. This does not mean you are not responsible for your actions. Each being bears responsibility for the choices they make, even if those choices are not made with full consciousness and mindfulness. However, accepting responsibility and making amends for harm you have caused is not the same as judging yourself for causing it.

Your Core Self is beyond all of the harm that has been caused to you and by you. It is the part of you that is closest to the ultimate Source of the Universe, and is the part of you that bears the closest resemblance to that Source. There is nothing of that Self that is worthy of condemnation or judgment; therefore, there is nothing of you that deserves these things.

You are more than the sum of your parts. At your core, you are an aspect of the Universe itself. This aspect deserves to live, to grow, to shine. Most importantly, it deserves to heal.

A Reflection of the Universe

*N*othing which has occurred in your life has truly changed you. You have changed, yes, but those changes were not created by others or by events. Those changes come from within you.

When harm occurs, it does alter how you see the world. It alters how you see yourself. And these things cause it to appear that you yourself have been altered.

Within you is the Core, the shining light around which your physical form was created. This Core, this light, has not been dulled or damaged. This light still shines within you, and although you might not see it, it shines brightly for those who truly see.

Know that this light is there, and know that you carry it regardless of harm your past has caused you. Seek this light within you, for that is the first step toward seeing it within others. Know this light is there, and embrace it, for some of you fear it instead.

Know your true self, and healing shall occur.

Each being, each living thing, is created by the Ultimate Source. Some may call this sentience the Universe, or God, or Creator. Humans have given it myriad names, but all names refer to the same Source. We shall primarily use the terms "Source" and "Universe" in these writings but invite you to mentally replace those words with the one that works best for you as you read.

Some of you reading this believe in no Source or higher power, and that is equally valid. Perhaps this chapter will not serve you, and you would benefit from moving on to the next rather than reading something which may cause you frustration or cognitive dissonance. We have no wish to upend your world view or perceptions of the Universe. We merely speak from what we know and have perceived and have no desire to enforce this knowledge and perception upon those who do not wish to hear it.

This Source, as some humans say, does not make errors. However, those humans who use that phrase use it to justify hatred and discrimination and do not recognize the fallacy of this. In truth, the fact that the Source makes no mistakes is indication that those who are transgender are truly so; those who are homosexual are truly so; and so forth. Having a body which does not match your mind is not a mistake on the part of the Source, and when one says the Source does not make mistakes, it proves that you are correct in knowing that your mind and body differ and this is how you were created.

Why, then, would Source create you with a mind and body that do not fit together? Why would Source create those whose existence will subject them to hatred and discrimination? Why would Source place someone in an environment in which they will experience harm?

These questions are understandable and necessary, yet even we, though existing in a plane closer to Source than your own, are unable to definitively answer, for we do not speak for that being. However, we can state that the Universe does not wish its creations to cause one another harm or pain. No one is created to be the recipient of such harm. No one is placed in any family or other environment with the purpose of experiencing hatred.

The Universe creates all beings as perfect and wondrous. Each of you is a reflection of the Universe itself, though not "created in its image" as some say, for Source has no physical form as humans perceive. It is, indeed, a being of energy, existing in a plane outside human comprehension. Your physical form, therefore, is not a reflection of it. The reflection is within you. The Core Self, or soul, or higher self; again, words are for your benefit, so we invite you to substitute the terms that work best for you for the ones we have chosen.

It may be said that you are created in the image Source holds in its mind, rather than in the image of Source itself.

No being is created with the intention of it experiencing pain or harm. No "soul contract" exists that requires you to be abused or traumatized. Your thoughts do not create these experiences. And Source does not wish its creations to be harmed. When one inflicts harm upon another, the Universe sorrows, much as a human parent might sorrow when their child commits an inappropriate act, for in some ways the Universe is a parent to all.

Source does not create abuse, nor does it place you intentionally in an environment where you will experience it. However, free will prevails even with the Ultimate Creator, for it cannot and will not interfere in the choices made by its creations. It does not wish its creations to be harmed, but it will not stop one who has chosen to inflict harm, for that would compromise free will. It does not create variations among humans so that one group may discriminate against another, but it will not prevent those who are determined to discriminate from doing so.

The Ultimate Source has its own will and makes its own choices, and it has granted this ability to all of its creations. This possession of free will is one of the ways in which all beings are created in the image of Source, for it has given us what it itself has.

Each being is perfect as created. The Universe sees no flaws or fallacies in its creations, merely differences. Some of these differences are less beneficial than others, but to the Universe, each quality and trait is valuable. Each being is valuable and valued.

If the Ultimate Creator itself views you as perfect and valued, how can you view yourself as less? Do you refute Source in its perceptions? Do you believe it is wrong or lying?

There are many cliches and statements among humans along these lines. Some are truthful and are meant to bring benefit. Others are yet another way in which humans attempt to dissuade one another from "thinking negatively" or to minimize or invalidate others' experiences. We do not make these statements for any of these reasons, but rather to encourage your thinking and perhaps guide you to a new way of viewing yourself.

You are not created to resemble Source, but rather in the image it holds of an ideal being. That is what "created in its image" accurately means. The image it has created rather than an exact replica of its appearance.

Perfection is a concept which some humans view with varying unpleasant emotions. This is understandable, for the idea of perfection has been twisted into something unattainable that is used to cause people to feel badly about themselves. This is not the original intention of the idea, nor is it an accurate interpretation.

Perfection simply means that there is no need to change anything about yourself. It means that as you were created, so shall you be. Bear in mind as you react to those words that you were not created having experienced harm and pain. You were created as an image of the Ultimate Source, one with knowledge, wisdom, and understanding that at times becomes locked away or buried once you are incarnate. You were created as Source wished you to be. This creation is not eliminated by anything you experience; the effects of your experiences merely overlay what was granted to you upon your initial creation.

Therefore, disliking those effects is acceptable. Wishing to correct behaviors and thought patterns that cause you problems is wise. But disliking your very Self and wishing to change that aspect is both unacceptable and unwise, for that Core Self is unchanged by your experiences and is the being you were created to be.

You may, of course, seek to change your Core Self. You may feel however you wish about who you are beneath all the layers left behind by your experiences. This, as with nearly everything in your life, is subject to your free will, and we will not tell you that you are not "allowed to" feel or think in any particular way. We strongly encourage you, however, to separate your experiences from who you are at your core, and to focus your dislike and your desire to change upon the effects of the experiences rather than your full Self.

If you would not view Source with the thoughts of "That sucks" or "That should change, it isn't right," why would you view yourself in those ways? Again, you are asked to separate your Self from the experiences you have had, for while those experiences have created impressions and behaviors, they have not altered who you truly are. They have merely obscured it from you. Seek to work on changing or eliminating the effects so that you may clearly see what lies beneath, rather than seeking to work on changing your entire Self, for the Core Self is perfect as it is, and you have the power to reconnect with this Self when you are progressing upon your healing journey.

Look around you. Many things, both natural and man-made, have what you might call flaws. A tree might have a broken branch, or a place where the bark has worn away, or leaves that are shredded. A bird may fly crookedly or be missing feathers. The desk at which River sits to type these words as we speak is covered with pockmarks and stains from decades of coffee cups and water glasses. Yet none of these things is imperfect. None requires "repair" or change.

So it is with you. When you view yourself, you cannot see what lies beneath the harm and damage that has been caused to you. You see only the pain you have suffered and the effects of what has been done, and you equate those things with who you are. This is why you so strongly desire to change yourself and why you experience feelings of dislike and hatred toward yourself, exacerbated, for some, by having been told by those who caused the harm that you deserved to be hurt and you should be disliked or hated for who you are.

Those people were lying to cause you further pain, and your view is now warped by their words and actions. You have internalized their treatment of you, and it has caused you to be unable to see yourself accurately, both literally and figuratively speaking.

If you believe the Ultimate Creator is wise and beautiful and perfect, and you believe nature to be the same despite some surface issues with some natural things, how can you believe yourself to be otherwise? Are you not part of nature? Are you not in the image of the Creator?

Some of you are having a negative emotional response as you read these words. However, even with that response, you recognize that the words are true, and this is causing dissonance for you.

When other humans have stated to you that you are not your experiences, in some cases they have used that phrasing to invalidate how you feel about what has occurred in your life. They have stated those things in an effort to cause you to cease talking about what has been done to you, because they are uncomfortable hearing what you say or because they, too, have had those words used against them in this way.

We do not seek to invalidate you in any way. Your feelings are valid, as are your memories of your experiences and your reactions to them. We are not attempting to tell you not to think about the past, nor are we saying you are unaffected by your experiences, for obviously those experiences have had an effect.

Rather, we are asking you to remember that despite the effects, despite what you see when you look in a mirror, despite the loss of connection between your conscious self and your Core Self, you are as beautiful and perfect as the Creator and its other creations. That beauty and perfection have not been altered or eliminated by your experiences. The effects of what you have experienced in your life are on the surface. As you heal, you will reconnect with your deeper Self and will see that that Self has not been altered. Your perceptions have been. Your behaviors and thought patterns have been. But your ultimate, deepest Self has not.

You are not being asked or told to pretend that nothing about you necessitates change. Only to believe that who you truly are is beautiful and perfect as it is. The surface things, the thoughts and behaviors and misperceptions, are what may need to be changed, though of course whether to change it is entirely your choice.

All things you do or do not do are subject to choice, despite your statements that you "have to" or "shouldn't" do certain things. "Have to" and "shouldn't" are not entirely accurate; what most humans mean when using those phrases is that the alternatives are frightening, potentially harmful, or otherwise unfeasible. That does not mean alternatives don't exist, but rather that the alternatives are not something they are willing to consider.

You do not "have to" change. You are choosing to do so, even if the reason for your choice is that no other alternative seems beneficial or workable for you. You do not have to view yourself as an aspect or image of the Ultimate Creator, but we encourage you to make that mental shift if you are able. You do not have to cease treating yourself with scorn and hatred, but ceasing would bring you greater benefit than continuing to treat yourself poorly.

The Universe has created you, and you are, at your core, as you are meant to be. However, each occurrence in your life, whether positive or negative, overlays part of your Core Self. You begin to equate yourself with your experiences and those overlays rather than with your Core. This is not due to any conscious decision you have made. Humans often believe they are what they do and what is done to them; it is simply the nature of humanity.

We tell you that you are not those experiences. You are not the overlying pieces that have obscured your Core Self. That Core is who you truly are, even if you have lost connection with it over the course of this incarnate lifetime.

The Universe is beautiful in all its aspects. Source is perfect. The natural world you see around you is beautiful and perfect even if it contains flaws and danger as well. Indeed, this balance between beauty and danger, between light and shadow, is present in all things and all beings, even the Ultimate Source. As a reflection or an image of Source, these things are likewise present in you.

Your role is not to eliminate the aspects of the Universe that you dislike or fear. Doing this would change the Universe intrinsically. It would not be what you have come to know, and may even cease to exist, for without balance existence is impossible. You see the beauty of the Universe even as you see the aspects you consider negative, so how is it that you do not see the beauty of yourself? Why is it that you seek to eliminate aspects of yourself?

Although your Core Self is not changed by your experiences, the ways in which you present yourself to the world are. When those ways cause problems or harm to others, learning alternative ways of operating is wise. However, seeking to eliminate those ways and aspects simply because they are not "light" or positive is unwise, for just as the Universe itself requires balance to exist, so do you. By endeavoring to eliminate any aspect of yourself, you are negating the whole you, for those aspects formed in response to what you experienced. They are part of you. You have been negated enough by others; refrain from doing so to yourself.

Indeed, consider the things you say to and about yourself. As the one saying them, and as one who is likely used to hearing them from others, you may not recognize the harm they cause. View them as if you were saying them to another person. Are they things you would state to a friend or loved one, or even a stranger? If someone told you those things were being said to them, would you point out the harm and the falseness?

If you would not say these things to anyone else and would tell others who heard these things that they are harmful and false, why do you perpetuate the harm to yourself? You are being harmed by them as much as any other would be, and you deserve it no more than they do.

In some human spiritual paths, each being is considered divine unto themself, for those paths recognize that Source has created each of us in its image, which includes an image of its divinity. You are a divine being. You are a reflection of the Universe itself. You are not any of the insults and negations you have heard or have spoken to yourself. None of those things can be true, for if they are not true of the Universe, how could they be true of you?

Know that you are perfect. Beneath the detritus of harm, pain, and insults, you are the perfect, beautiful creation first envisioned by Source. The changes your experiences have caused run deep, but not as deep as your Core Self. Not as deep as the qualities the Creator has instilled in you. As you read these words for the first time, you may not yet be in a place where you are able to see your own beauty and perfection. You may have lost connection with your Core Self. But those things are there, and you may regain them through your healing journey if you choose.

Nothing which has occurred in your life has truly changed you. You have changed, yes, but those changes were not created by others or by events. Those changes come from within you.

When harm occurs, it does alter how you see the world. It alters how you see yourself. And these things cause it to appear that you yourself have been altered.

However, no one can take away who and what you are. Your power has not been stolen; it has merely been hidden from you. As you progress in your journey, you will uncover it, for with each step in healing, some of the detritus is removed, clearing the way for you to see yourself as you truly are. A beautiful, powerful, wonderful creation.

Create Balance

*T*he aim of embarking upon a healing journey is not to eliminate all memories and effects of your experiences. Nor is it to eliminate the emotions you feel about those experiences, even the emotions humans deem negative. The purpose of healing is not to deny or remove shadows or inner children. It is to learn to embrace and work with them.

In some spiritual spheres, humans have begun to inaccurately state such things as "only positive vibes; you get what you put out" and "if you think negative thoughts you get negative things." These statements are false. While your energetic vibration does affect what comes into your life, a high vibration does not automatically equate to positivity. Nor are your thoughts the only things which affect your vibration.

Those who speak these words may truly believe them. However, some are aware that they are false and yet continue to propagate them so that they may feel better about themselves in some ways. They have been negated and invalidated by these platitudes and, out of their own pain, seek to invalidate and negate others.

Every sentient being, including the Ultimate Creator, carries both light and darkness. The entire Universe is based upon the concept of balance, as is your natural world. Without darkness, there is no daytime. Without light, there is no night. Both must exist in balance. Both are necessary for existence.

Such it is with you and your healing journey. Seeking to eliminate your inner "darkness" only prolongs the pain from your past experiences. Those who harmed you sought to eliminate facets of you. If you do the same, you are furthering that harm. Denying the existence of your shadow self or your inner children does not remove them. It merely proves to them that no human, yourself included, may be trusted, and that they must fight and continue causing harm in order to validate their existence.

As you work toward a more beneficial life, know that all aspects and facets of you are not only valid, but needed. Anger, as an example, is not a harmful, negative thing. It is a signal to you that your needs are being ignored or that someone is causing harm to you. It is a warning sign that something must change. And it is a valid emotion, for when you are harmed or negated, you are not expected to simply nod, smile, and acknowledge it. It is valid and appropriate to feel anger at those times.

The potential inappropriateness and harm of emotions comes from how you choose to express them, not from the feeling and acknowledgement of them. Although your emotions are valid, actions you take in response may not be. If your reaction to anger is to lash out with loud, damaging words or physical violence, this is not appropriate, for you are causing harm to the one toward whom you are lashing out. The anger itself is valid and appropriate, but your expression of it is not.

These difficult emotions and their inappropriate expression often come from what humans may call their shadows or their inner children. These are facets of yourself that were splintered off and frozen at times of trauma. Although some people refer to them as separate entities, they are in fact one and the same. Your shadows are your inner children, or are the emotions and reactions that come from those children.

Each time a human experiences trauma, their consciousness splinters, and a piece of consciousness is frozen at that moment in time. This piece does not age as the person does, but because it remains part of the person, it impacts how the person thinks and acts. At times, you speak of feeling young or of "acting like a child." That is because a fragment of your consciousness still is a child. Possibly more than one.

Just as you would not eliminate a toddler who has misbehaved out of ignorance of appropriate ways, it is unnecessarily cruel to attempt to eliminate your inner children. These frozen consciousnesses need instruction and guidance in proper behavior, but more than that, they need the love and compassion you did not receive when you were the age at which they became frozen. They need you to be for them what no one was for you.

Of course this is a difficult task for many survivors of trauma, and that is why so many speak of eliminating their shadows. It is easier to eliminate or deny them than to feel love and compassion for them, particularly as they are the parts of you that received the trauma and therefore you may blame them for what occurred, much as the one who inflicted the harm likely blamed you. But no part of you is responsible for what was done. If you would not blame a separate child for being abused or traumatized, why then would you blame the child you once were? They did not cause what happened. They—you—are not to blame.

Keeping patience with these frozen consciousnesses may prove difficult. Even things that would not cause you to lose your patience with a flesh-and-blood child may cause a loss of patience with your inner children. This is understandable. Their actions directly affect you, for their actions, to all appearances, are your actions. What you do and say that is spurred by these inner children impacts your relationships with others and with yourself.

Feeling impatient or angry with the frozen consciousnesses is understandable and is not wrong. However, speaking harshly to them is speaking harshly to yourself, which is something undesirable. You have heard harsh words and insults from others. There is no benefit to projecting them upon yourself.

In managing your emotions, balance is necessary. In addressing your darker aspects, balance is of benefit. And in learning to manage and work with your inner children, you will also require balance. When one teaches a toddler, the aim is to both inform the child what behavior is unacceptable and teach them acceptable behaviors. This is likewise the best course to take with your inner children. These aspects of yourself do not know how to navigate the world effectively and beneficially. You, the conscious adult self, must teach them.

We wish to clarify that although we speak of these frozen consciousnesses as separate from you, in truth they are not. They are simply aspects of your personality and yourself. This is not the same as what some humans term "multiple personalities" or "dissociative identity disorder," for those are clinical states in which one's psyche has fragmented into consciousnesses that are separate from one another and act as individual beings. Frozen consciousnesses, as we speak of them, are not separate. They do not cause the conscious self to lose time or memories, and do not take over control of the body for any period of time. Rather, they exert influence over the conscious self's actions and words without taking over.

However, although these frozen consciousnesses are not separate from you, some of you may find healing easier if you temporarily consider them as such. When River began working with this concept, they struggled to release their anger toward their inner children for having been victims of the experiences that spawned them. Although River acknowledged they would not feel such anger or project such blame toward actual children who had had similar experiences, they were unable to release the anger and blame they felt toward themself, which extended to projecting it to their inner children.

When we suggested to River that they treat their inner children temporarily as separate beings, they found it easier to release the emotions that held them back from their healing journey. They were able to accept the children and nurture them in ways they themself had not been treated when they were a child, and indeed in ways they found it difficult to nurture their flesh-and-blood children. Through listening to and acknowledging what their inner children said to them rather than negating it or meeting it with anger, River was able to form a connection that brought these frozen consciousnesses into fuller integration with River's conscious self.

Although River still at times refers to these inner children as separate beings, for the most part they no longer consider them as such. Rather than having verbal conversations with the "children" and having to instruct them, River works in concert with them. They are able now to perceive and accept those pieces of themself as truly being part of them, and their healing has progressed accordingly.

These consciousnesses do not comprehend balance or the need for it, for they operate on almost a purely emotional level. However, you, as your conscious self, operate from both emotion and reason.

Striking the balance between these two is important in your healing journey, and helping your inner children find this balance is vital.

No emotions that you feel are incorrect or wrong. No emotions that you feel will create negatives in your life or cause worse things to happen, although some humans state that this is so. Some even state that their guides say this; we will not refute that notion, but will note that guides are with you to help you to improve your life and to show you support and compassion. The idea that you are not allowed to feel the full range of human emotions is not supportive and is in fact harmful, so we question whether guides have said this or whether the humans relaying the information have misunderstood or are speaking filtered through their own beliefs.

However, it is not for us to say that any being is wrong. We are collaborating on this work to express our beliefs and perceptions and to offer encouragement to those of you who have been harmed by others in the past and are being harmed at this time by those who purport to tell you how to manage your trauma. It is not the place of anyone to tell you what is and isn't acceptable to feel or to think. People may tell you that your outward expression of those emotions and thoughts is unacceptable, and that is valid if they are affected by it. But within yourself, only you can determine what is and is not appropriate.

If you are feeling only unpleasant emotions or are thinking only upsetting or harmful thoughts, this is an imbalance. An imbalance interferes with your healing journey and at times with your very functioning in your life. If you are experiencing this type of imbalance, you are encouraged to seek aid from a human professional as well as from your guides. Although we as guides have access to a far broader range of knowledge than any human, we are not trained in the specialties of human health care and are therefore not qualified to treat you. Your guides can and will assist you with your struggles, but they may also encourage you to seek professional aid.

As you grow and progress in your healing journey and your life as a whole, you are encouraged to seek balance in all areas. Your very existence is part of the balance of the Universe. If you are out of balance, so is the Universe as a whole. If you reject or negate aspects of yourself, you bring imbalance.

You are wholly deserving of love and of existence. We ask that you remember this.

Vibration and Creation

Many humans speak of vibration. "Positive vibes only," some say, or "Raise your vibration by thinking only positive thoughts."

This reflects a great misunderstanding of what some humans have titled the "Law of Attraction." It also reflects a lack of understanding of energy and energetic vibration. Although this chapter's information is not exclusive to those who have experienced harm and trauma, we include it here because we are aware that many of you have been further harmed by the incorrect statements of these concepts and principles.

All beings, indeed all things whether living or nonliving and whether natural or manmade, are surrounded by their own individual field of energy. This field varies depending upon what it surrounds; although energy is energy, the structure and form of the energetic field is not the same for all beings and things.

Throughout your existence, your energetic field is affected by occurrences. The effects are present whether you experience physical or emotional incidents, for energy does not differentiate. The specific effects may be different depending upon whether they are caused by something physical or emotional, but there will be an effect. Likewise, what the energetic field experiences or receives will affect your physical and mental/emotional well-being.

Your energetic field vibrates at a certain frequency. This frequency may be felt by others, and if their energetic vibration is greatly different from yours, you and they will experience dissonance. This is why at times you may meet someone to whom you take an instant dislike, or who immediately feels "off" to you. It is due to a mismatch between your energetic vibrations.

Similarly, they may experience a reaction to your vibration. At times, this is the root cause of abuse or other harm. They lash out against the discomfort or pain they feel as a result of the energetic mismatch. This is particularly true if your vibration is higher than theirs, for a high vibration will cause discomfort or pain to one whose vibration is lower. This, in fact, is why those of us who serve as guides to humans may only work with humans whose energetic vibrations are of certain levels, for although no human's vibration can ever be as high as a guide's, if the incompatibility is too great, our vibration will cause you pain or harm. We wish to avoid this.

Humans often equate high vibration with "good" and low with "bad" or "negative." However, this is not the case and is where the misunderstandings and misinterpretations arise.

Energetic frequency is neither good nor bad. It is simply a thing which exists. River often uses the example of an FM radio dial, which is something that is comprehensible to them and to many other humans. On that dial, one station may be at a low frequency, such as 88.3, while another may be at a high frequency, such as 107.9. This difference in frequency does not mean that one station is better or worse than the other, nor does it mean that the station at higher frequency is good while the station at lower frequency is bad. They are simply different.

Such it is with energetic vibration. The frequency at which one's energy field vibrates is neither better nor worse than the frequency at which another's vibrates. They are simply different.

Therefore, the oft-stated precept of "Positive vibes only" does not guarantee high energetic vibration. Your vibration is not automatically positive when it is high, nor do positive thoughts automatically create higher vibration.

It is, indeed, possible for someone who lives with conditions such as trauma or depression, and who therefore thinks negative thoughts and struggles to find any happiness or joy, to have a higher vibrational frequency than someone who endeavors to dismiss any unpleasant thought or emotion. This is in part because dismissing or denying things that you find unpleasant is itself an act which can lower vibration through negation or dishonesty about what you think and feel. It is also because thoughts and emotions are not the only factors which determine the frequency of one's energetic vibration.

Everything you experience in your life, whether it comes from internal sources or external, affects your energy system. Your energy field and energy centers—what some call chakras—may be damaged, blocked, or unbalanced due to illness, injuries, or even harsh words spoken by another. These are not the only factors which impact the energy system, but are the most prominent.

When your energy system receives any type of damage or imbalance, your frequency is lowered. If the flow of energy through your system is impeded by tears in the field, or imbalance in the energy centers, or any other factor, the energy does not vibrate at optimal frequency because the vibration is created by the flow. Thinking negative thoughts does not necessarily damage your energy system. It does not necessarily impede the flow of energy, and therefore may not affect your vibrational frequency at all.

Your energetic vibration is not a static, fixed thing. It can be raised or lowered at any time. We have noted some ways in which it might be lowered. Raising it can be as simple as stating, with intention and focus, "I intend to raise my vibration to higher and higher levels." Your vibration may also be raised through practices that repair and restore your energy system, such as energy healing or certain spiritual practices such as meditation or yoga. Spending time in activities or with people who enable you to feel happiness and joy will raise your vibration as well.

Thoughts and emotions can influence your vibration, but they don't always cause any alteration in your vibrational frequency, and they are far from the only possible influences. Indeed, thoughts and emotions are less influential in the level of your vibrational frequency than most other factors. Thinking negative thoughts or speaking negative statements does not necessarily create low vibration in you, though if those thoughts and statements cause harm, they may lower both your vibration and the vibration of the one who is harmed by them.

The so-called "Law of Attraction" teaches that you bring to you what you put out into the world. Many humans interpret this to mean that if you think negative thoughts, you will create negative occurrences in your life, and extend this to blame recipients of harm by stating that they must have magnetized the abuse and harm into their lives by not thinking positively enough.

This is not the true meaning of this principle, and is not how it was originally presented to humans. However, as with many things, some subtleties and meanings are lost in translation, as it were. No matter how a principle is presented to humans, their presentation in turn will be affected by their perceptions and understanding. This is why so many teachings of spiritual or religious nature have diverged from their original meaning and are utilized, whether intentionally or not, to cause harm.

When we say that you attract what you put out, that does not refer to your thoughts and words, but rather to your energetic vibration. You draw to you people and experiences of compatible vibration. If your vibration is low, you will draw others of low vibration, and these others may cause you harm or you may also attract harmful experiences that have a low frequency and cause your vibration to become lower still. If your vibration is high, you will attract others of high vibration and experiences that are at a high frequency.

To attract beneficial people and experiences into your life, it is useful to raise your vibration. But again, your vibration is not affected solely, or even primarily, by your thoughts or emotions, and denying yourself the right to feel your full range of emotions and tend to your thoughts will actually result in a lower vibration than allowing yourself to feel, think, and speak all emotions and thoughts in nonharmful ways.

There is no need for "positive vibes only," because negative thoughts, in and of themselves, do not lower your vibration. Positive vibration is not synonymous with high vibration; negative vibration is not synonymous with low. As with everything in a human life, balance is necessary. The more balanced your life is, both externally and within, the higher your vibrational frequency will be, and the more beneficial and abundant your life will become.

Those who state otherwise in teaching the Law of Attraction are not acting out of malice, for the most part, nor out of a desire to invalidate others. They genuinely believe they are interpreting this precept correctly, perhaps because it is what they were taught by someone they trust or consider an authority on the subject. However, when they state this precept in ways that invalidate others or blame others for their own harmful experiences, these people are lowering their own vibrations. Negation and invalidation of any form is something which will lower the vibrational frequency.

Negative thoughts or emotions do not beget negative occurrences. Energy is not attracted to thoughts, emotions, words, or actions. It is attracted to energy. Each thing you think, feel, say, or do in your life does affect your energetic vibration, and therefore it is wise to be mindful of those things. It is wise also to be mindful of judging others or of condemning them for not thinking positively or "having only positive vibes," for judgment and condemnation lower your own vibration.

You have seen in your world that people who cause harm to others, people who hate or who spread malice, receive abundance and benefit. If the Law of Attraction were actually that negative thoughts, words, and actions lower vibration, these people would have some of the lowest energetic frequencies possible and would therefore attract only pain and harm to themselves. Yet this is not the case. They receive abundance while others, those who appear to only think, feel, and speak positively, receive harm and painful experiences.

How, then, can this be if it is true that positivity raises the vibration and negativity lowers it? If you attract positive things through positivity, and negative things through negativity, how can those who spread negativity and commit harmful actions receive greater benefit and positive experiences than those who believe they are spreading positivity?

As you may have determined, it is because thoughts, words, and actions, no matter how harmful or how beneficial, are not the sole determinants of energetic vibrational frequency. Someone who is malicious and spreads hatred and harm may have a higher vibration than someone who speaks and thinks positively because there are other factors involved.

This book is not intended as a treatise on energy and vibrational frequency, nor do we wish to dissect all of the many factors that contribute to the frequency of one's vibration. That would be another book unto itself, one on which we may request River's collaboration with us in the future. For the current volume, we seek merely to disabuse some of you of the notion that you are not allowed to think unpleasant thoughts or feel uncomfortable emotions. We seek also to refute the victim-blaming that so often results from the miscomprehension of the Law of Attraction.

No matter what you have thought, what you have said or done, or what you feel, nothing about you has caused the harm you have received from others. Your vibrational frequency may have been low enough to attract those who harmed you or the experiences themselves, but you did not cause your vibration to be low through not being positive enough. That idea is illogical and false. You are not the sole determinant of the level of your energetic vibration, because it is affected by things both within your control and not.

We are saddened by the harm some of you have received through the misapplication of the concept of energetic attraction. We sorrow at the pain that is caused when people misuse the principle to blame others for receiving harm rather than placing responsibility upon those who committed the harm.

Over time, it is our hope that humans will gain fuller and more accurate comprehension of this precept. In the meanwhile, we hope that this chapter has given some of you the understanding that you did not create what was done to you by somehow choosing a low vibration, and we hope that you recognize that no emotion, thought, word, or action is wrong or unacceptable so long as no one is harmed by it. Even those things that humans deem negative are not unacceptable and will not cause you to have a horrible life.

Feel as you feel. Speak what you wish to speak, particularly if you are doing so in order to facilitate your healing journey. Think the thoughts that enter your mind and acknowledge them even if they appear negative. Remember that the intention needs to be harming none, and know that thinking, feeling, and saying these things will not cause bad things to happen to you, for that is not how the Universe works.

You attract people and things with energetic vibrations that are compatible with yours. This is true whether your vibrational frequency is low or high. Learning to raise your vibration through certain activities will benefit you, but you are not responsible for who or what comes to you in response to your frequency. You are not responsible for what others do when they are in your life.

You do have the power to create a beneficial life for yourself. You have the power to change your vibrational frequency. All of this power lies within you, but if you have been unaware that you hold the power, you have not been using it. Those who have told you that you created the harm you experienced are wrong. Those who have told you that you cause negative occurrences in your life by thinking negatively or feeling negative emotions are wrong.

Humans have had an understanding of some of what you call metaphysical principles for millennia, but the level of understanding waxes and wanes through the years. You are in a time now when understanding is increasing and people are becoming more aware and mindful of the possibilities, yet full understanding is not yet present. Some people embrace concepts and principles they do not fully comprehend, and when this occurs, they spread their misunderstandings and misperceptions. As stated, most of them do not do this out of malice, but merely out of ignorance of the true nature of the principles.

We do not purport to speak all the truth of the Universe. We do not claim to be the ultimate authorities on the Law of Attraction or any other concepts we discuss within this book. However, we do state that humans have vastly misinterpreted some Universal principles and concepts and have utilized their misinterpretations to blame and shame others for what they have experienced. This is not a valid course of action. Blaming and causing others to feel shame does not aid healing. It is not a demonstration of love or compassion. Whether the intention to harm is there or not, this course of action does cause harm.

To those of you who have been harmed by this misstatement of the principles of energetic attraction, to those who have concluded that you are to blame for your experiences or that you are beyond help or healing because you are unable to stop feeling and thinking certain things, we tell you that what you have been taught previously is wrong. You are not to blame. You are not beyond help or healing. You have every right to think as you think and feel as you feel, and these thoughts and feelings will not cause you further harm or attract unpleasant people or things into your life.

Allowing your thoughts and feelings to exist as they are, and acknowledging them and the parts of you from which they arise, is essential to your healing journey. It is also one way to raise your energetic vibration, which will bring greater abundance and joy into your life.

If these words and thoughts do not resonate for you, you may reject them. If you feel truth in them, you may reject the other things you have been told on the subject. The choice of what to believe and how to proceed from here is entirely yours.

We leave this chapter with this thought: Energy is everywhere and vibrates at varying frequencies. You are part of everywhere and everything. You matter, and you deserve an abundant life, even when other humans tell you otherwise. No human knows everything; indeed, no being save the Ultimate Creator knows everything. It is a learning process, and it is our hope that as you learn other, more compassionate and productive ways of interpreting the laws of energetic attraction, you will share these with those who have likewise been harmed by the misinterpretations. As you heal, you will spread healing.

You Have the Right to Heal

*T*here are those among you who question your own healing process. Who wonder whether you have the right to remove from your life those who have harmed you. Who wonder whether you have the right to be traumatized by your experiences when you believe others have had it worse.

Beloveds, you have the right to do whatever it is you need in order to heal, so long as no one is intentionally harmed by your choices.

Removing people from your life may be met with accusations of harm, but these are the faint cries of those who are angry that you have placed yourself in a position of priority in your own life. These accusations come from the people who believe that family must be forgiven regardless of what has occurred but are unable or unwilling to extend that forgiveness to others.

No one has an automatic right to a place in your life. No one has a claim on your existence, your mind, your heart. Who they are to you is irrelevant. If they have harmed you, they do not belong around you, for on some level their very presence causes further harm.

Should you choose to remove people from your life, to cut ties with them, you will receive judgment. Some people will refuse to accept that you are allowed to place restrictions on who is permitted to be in your life. Some people will enter the fray, so to speak, because they enjoy drama or believe they have the right to an opinion and to enforce their beliefs about something in which they have no direct involvement.

This judgment may be difficult for you to face, but we encourage you to stand fast in your decisions. If you allow someone who has harmed you to continue to be present in your life, they will continue to cause harm. If you remove them but allow them back based upon the judgment and comments of others, you are causing harm to yourself, for once you have chosen to remove them, if they return, it is your choice.

You have the right to heal as you see fit. You have the right to allow only those who are supportive and caring to have access to you. You have the right to deny anyone at all a place in your life, for it is your life even if you have been led to believe otherwise.

Healing is not possible without first recognizing and accepting the power that lies within you. This is not power to hold over any other person, but rather an innate power with which you were born that enables you to create your life and to manage how you live. This power is often said to have been "taken away" or "stolen" at times of trauma. However, the power has not been removed from you even if you feel as though it has. Rather, it is dormant, hidden even from yourself in order to keep yourself safe, for showing power to an abuser can result in further abuse.

However, when you embark upon your healing journey, you must call forth that power. Without it, you cannot choose the changes which occur in your life and you will struggle to accept the changes that come. This power is an intrinsic part of you and cannot be taken away, but after long periods of forgetting it is there and not utilizing it, you must learn anew how to use it for your benefit.

One of the first steps in calling forth your inner power is creating a life of safety and boundaries. This includes cutting people from your life if they are harmful or toxic to you or if they oppose rather than support your healing journey. You do have the power to determine how your life is structured and who fits within that structure. Allow yourself to experience your inner power by exercising it in determining who is permitted to remain in your life.

For some of you, power is a difficult concept, for you have seen it misused by those who believe power is something to hold over others rather than to hold within themselves. You fear that if you allow yourself to accept and use your own power, you, also, will misuse it. This is a valid fear, for you learn what is demonstrated to you. If you have seen only misuse and abuse of power and have not seen power used for benefit, you will at first struggle to determine how to use your inner power properly.

However, this struggle does not preclude your beneficial use of your power. It merely means that mindfulness must accompany each attempt you make. Without mindfulness, it is indeed likely that you may inadvertently cause harm. You are unlikely to use your power mindlessly, though. Your awareness of the possibilities will keep your consciousness and intentions focused as you learn to embrace and use this power.

Power is not something one holds over another. When one uses what they call power to subjugate others, to bring harm, or to enforce their beliefs and desires, this is not true power. It is, rather, force. It is ego. It brings no benefit to any, not even to the one who does these things, for within themselves they know they are causing harm, and this harm will come back to them at some point.

When you have been on the receiving end of such a misuse of power, it is difficult to believe that there is another way. It is difficult to conceive of having and using power yourself. But again, we tell you that "power" held over another is not truly power. Power is something that exists within each being and is used by that being over themself alone. Subjugation, authoritarianism, force, abuse…none of these is power.

We encourage you to recognize and embrace what power truly means. We encourage you to see that you have true power within you, and this power can benefit you and others when you are ready to learn to work with it. Your ego may arise and attempt to steer your use of power toward subjugation of others, but you know the truth of what power is and will not allow your ego to control your use of it. You have nothing to fear within yourself, though we know that having experienced traumatic events, you find it difficult to trust yourself.

This power, the true power within you, is essential for your healing journey. When you are unable to accept that you have the power to heal, you will find yourself unable to heal. You will resist.

You will put the focus upon others for your difficulties. You will state that your power was stolen and therefore you cannot use it. All of these responses are because you will not accept the power that is there, not because the power does not exist.

For some of you, this is the step that will take the longest. Hesitation to embrace your inner power is understandable given your experiences, and we do not seek to minimize what you have lived through or the effects those things have had upon you. You have become conditioned to viewing everything as a threat, for this is what your brain tells you due to the experiences you have had. This alteration, this "rewiring" as River terms it, is not something you chose and cannot be undone simply by wishing it away.

Because you view so many things as a threat, it is understandable that you view even yourself as a threat under certain circumstances. Power is frightening to you; the possibility that you hold power within yourself is even more frightening. Additionally, as you read these words, some of you are responding defensively. You are insisting to yourself—for although you address your words to us, they are truly aimed toward yourself—that your power was actually stolen, that we do not know what we are saying, that we are wrong.

Deeper within, though, you feel the truth of our words, and it is this which gives rise to the negative reactions. You know that it is true, and that is terrifying to you, and it causes you to wonder what sort of person you are that you have rejected this power for so long.

This is not a judgment upon you. It is no flaw of yours that has caused you to reject or not recognize your inner power. It is the direct result of the trauma inflicted upon you. The only type of person you are is human, with all the various things that means. We do not judge and encourage you to also refrain from judgment.

Healing is not something to accomplish and move on. It is not a destination, but rather a journey, one which is likely to last the remainder of your incarnation and possibly beyond. It is something which takes time, although some say time is unnecessary and one should be able to "just get over" what has occurred in one's life.

This line of thought is both harmful and impossible. When one has experienced harm at the hands of others, when one's entire life has been built upon receiving and attempting to avoid this harm, healing is far from simple. It is not solely a matter of changing how one thinks, but indeed of rewiring the mind to correct the alterations made by the trauma. This is no easy task, nor is it for those who believe it should be easy. It is a task, rather, that necessitates time, tolerance, and courage.

In some cases, those who preach that one should "just get over" trauma, those who claim that it is indeed as simple as thinking differently, are themselves on healing journeys. They are learning what will work. They are learning that there is no shame in needing time. Perhaps they are combatting denial and anger at what has occurred in their lives, and they state these things out of a wish that they were true rather than believing they actually are.

This makes their statements no less invalidating or harmful to others, but it does indicate that perhaps compassion toward them and their journeys will serve a greater purpose than arguing with them or refuting their words. They, too, are learning, and they, too, will need time. We are not advising that you excuse their words. You need not excuse harmful behavior. We are simply suggesting that you view these people with compassion in addition to any other emotions their words bring to rise in you.

To heal, it is necessary to recognize that healing is a process that may not reach full fruition in this lifetime. It is necessary to accept that whatever amount of time you need is valid and acceptable, and that no other being has the right to tell you how to heal or how long to take. Most importantly, it is necessary to believe that healing is possible, for without belief, you will be unwilling to take the steps required in this journey.

You have a right to heal from your experiences. No matter what has occurred in your past, you are not obligated to remain in the energy and mindset left by those events. You have the right to learn new ways of operating in the world that accommodate the changes trauma has made in your brain while allowing you to live a full life. Needing these accommodations and adjustments is not a sign of weakness or of unwillingness to heal; it is no different from someone with physical limitations requiring modifications in order to accomplish tasks or maneuver around a physical environment.

You have a right to determine how you wish to proceed with

your healing journey. You need not discuss it with anyone if you do not wish to do so, though we encourage you to seek aid and support from those with whom you are close as well as from one who is trained in facilitating this type of healing. Seeking help and support, and seeking professional services, is also not a sign of weakness or of an expectation that someone else will do the work for you. It is natural to require assistance for any task, particularly one as broad and intensive as working to heal from traumatic events.

You have a right to choose what path and processes work best for you in your journey. Things that work for others may not work for you. That does not render them right and you wrong, or vice versa. It simply means that no one else is you, and you are no one else. This journey, regardless of how much support you receive, is a very individualized one, and it is valid to use the tools that are viable for you rather than accepting someone else's statements of what "should" work based upon what worked for them.

This includes medications. Some practitioners who label themselves "spiritual" preach that medication should be avoided at all costs. They share images stating that medication is poison and nature is the cure for all ills. That is their belief and they are entitled to it, but we wish you to know that there is no harm or shame in taking medicines that aid you in building and maintaining your health and well-being, whether that is physical or mental. If you find that medication works for you and supports your healing, you may ignore those who state that you are wrong or weak for taking it. This is your journey, not theirs, and you have a right to use the tools which work for you, whatever those may be.

Some of those who work as coaches, healing practitioners, and in other practices and methods that facilitate healing have experienced their own trauma. They seek to serve others in healing while still being on their own healing journeys. This is acceptable, for there is no need to be "fully healed" in order to help others. Indeed, the concept of being "fully healed" is a fallacy, for it is simply not possible in any given lifetime to heal all of the harm and pain one experiences. The necessity in becoming a practitioner who helps others heal is that you be on your own healing journey and that you have made sufficient progress that your struggles and the effects of your trauma do not cause impact to those you seek to assist.

Unfortunately, some of those who do this work have not done sufficient healing in these areas. They insist that their way of navigating their healing journeys is the only valid way. They assume that the things they have done in their healing journey are possible for everyone. They persist in telling others "You must try this! It works!" even when those others have not asked for advice or suggestions, under the guise of "wanting to alleviate suffering."

Some of you reading these words have engaged in some of the above behaviors. This is not a judgment upon you or any other. You are all human, and you behave as humans behave. At times, this includes having blinders on, as it were, to the reality that not everyone can heal as you do, not everyone can engage in the healing practices you utilize, and not everyone desires your assistance or advice.

While it is desirable to offer support and suggestions to others, particularly if your work involves aiding others in their healing journeys, you are encouraged to remember that what you have done for your own healing may not work for others. Your practices and choices may not be valid for everyone. Your advice and suggestions may be unwanted unless they have been requested.

The latter is particularly important to remember. If you offer unrequested suggestions about another's healing journey, you are violating their free will. You might say, "Oh, but they have the choice of whether to listen." That is true, but you have taken away their right to choose whether they wish to receive your input in the first place. We ask you to consider whether you would be pleased if someone gave advice to you without your consent and refused to accept your statements that you do not want the advice. Some of you have done exactly that to others and cannot understand why they are upset, or have determined that they do not wish to heal because they do not wish to receive your suggestions.

Many of those who have experienced trauma have experienced the denial and removal of their rights and free will. If you claim a wish to help others in their healing journeys from trauma and other experiences, how do you believe denying and removing their rights and free will can help them? You are doing to them what others have done. You are doing to them what may have been done to you.

You do carry knowledge and wisdom that will benefit others in their healing journeys. We do not state that you must keep those things to yourself. We say only that it is detrimental to share them without first obtaining the consent of the one with whom you wish to share, and it is even more detrimental to share your knowledge when another has expressed that they do not wish to receive it. If you wish to be of service to your fellow humans, refrain from engaging in detrimental practices in the name of "helping" them.

Similarly, when one has undergone their own healing journey and has found practices that work well for them, it is natural that they wish to share this information with others who are on healing journeys. But what has worked for one may not work for another. It is acceptable to share information once you have obtained consent from the person with whom you wish to share, but if they state something will not work for them, it is necessary to accept that response. They are not judging you or condemning your practice. They are assessing it for themself as something from which they may or may not benefit.

At times, someone who has undergone a healing journey becomes so enamored of a practice or technique that helped them that they refuse to listen when others say it will not work for them or they do not wish to try it. This person may then condemn those others as "not wanting to be well" or "being rude." They may insist that the others are simply refusing to listen or do not know what is best for them.

This is unfortunately frequent in certain spiritual communities and practices. Someone who has found something that aids them in their healing journey becomes convinced that it is the only way to heal and that others therefore must try it as well. They insist, and when they are met with refusal, they become aggressive and belligerent in their efforts. They become so convinced that they are right that they cannot and will not see that others may have different experiences. They take refusals as personal affronts and respond accordingly.

You are free to progress in your healing journey in whatever way works best for you, so long as no one is harmed by it. Others have this freedom as well. Sharing what you have learned or found is not problematic in and of itself, for you may reach others who are unaware of the practice and will benefit from it. However, sharing without first ascertaining that the other person wishes to hear what you have to say, or sharing when the other has stated they do not wish to hear it, serves no one. Becoming angry or arrogant when someone refutes your suggestion is not of service.

Some of you who read these words have experienced anger and negation from practitioners who believe their way of healing is the only correct way. You have been accused of not wanting to heal or of not knowing what is best for you.

We wish you to know that the anger and negation you have experienced is not your responsibility. You have done nothing wrong by not wishing to hear someone's suggestions or by knowing or believing that their suggestions would not work for you. The accusations made are false and are due to the other person's judgment, not to anything about you.

We invite you to consider whether one who attempts to force their beliefs and practices upon another is truly progressing on their healing journey. Consider, also, whether they are acting in a spiritual manner and in a way that will raise their energetic vibration, or whether their anger and belligerence are nonspiritual and will lower vibration. And if you are one who has attempted to push beliefs on others, we encourage you to consider the effect this behavior has on them and on you.

Each person has the right to find their own healing path. Each person is free to determine when or whether to embark upon that path. You are free to share information with others, but you are encouraged to do so in a way that honors their free will and their rights and freedoms.

You are also encouraged to honor your own free will and freedoms. Remember that no other human—indeed, no other being—can know you as well as you know yourself. If something that is suggested to you for healing does not resonate, you may reject it. If another person insists that their way is the right way to heal, you may choose not to listen and may cut ties with that person if they continue to insist. No matter who someone is, and no matter the qualifications they have or claim to have, no one knows better than you do what will truly work for you in your healing journey.

You are encouraged to embrace and honor this knowledge, for

true healing includes the regaining of the trust you once had in yourself. You may not even recall having had this trust, for it may have been dulled or removed before you can remember, but at some time in your life, you did trust yourself. Seek this state again as you consider and embark on your healing journey, for it will serve you far better than misplaced trust in those who only speak from their own experience and are unwilling to consider that others may experience things differently.

Patience In Healing

*R*ecognizing that you have aspects in need of healing does not cause the healing to occur. Work will be necessary on your part in order to alter the patterns and changes caused by the traumatic experiences you have endured. This work will not be easy, nor will it be fast.

At times as you progress in your journey, you may feel as if you are making no progress at all. Indeed, at times you may appear, to your own perception, to be regressing. These times are difficult and painful, and some people give up rather than continuing.

We wish you to know that healing is a process, not an instantaneous occurrence. Once you begin your healing journey, some steps you take will be large and others small. Some steps will be forward while others seem to keep you in place or take you backward. Some steps may be accomplished in short amounts of time while others feel as if they are taking a lifetime. And in fact, some may actually take a lifetime to complete.

We do not say this to discourage you, but rather to offer encouragement, for all of these things are typical in a healing journey. Being "stuck" in one place does not last forever. You will move forward again. Regressing does not mean you aren't healing or that you are more damaged than you realized. It simply means that the healing journey is never straightforward. At some point, you will begin to progress again rather than regressing.

However, at times when you feel stagnant or seem to be regressing, you may feel as if that time will last forever. You may reach a point of despair at which you believe you will never heal or progress further. Perhaps you will even believe you deserve to feel this way.

No human deserves to feel hopeless. No one deserves to feel as if they cannot be better. Regardless of your experiences, you do not deserve to feel this way. You deserve to progress.

During the experiences which led to your trauma, you likely were told that you were a bad person who deserved bad things. Those who harmed you may have stated that they only did so because of what kind of person you were. They may have told you that you were incapable of doing anything correctly or anything in which to take pride.

They spoke words of negation, hatred, and harm because of the issues within themselves. What they said to you was false. They wished to diminish and destroy you out of the hatred and pain they carried within. In belittling others, they believed they found superiority and a way to stop the feelings and beliefs they had about themselves.

This, of course, does not work. One cannot heal by wounding others. One cannot eliminate pain by inflicting it.

Being on the receiving end of that behavior, however, causes its own pain and wounds. No matter what the reason the person had for inflicting harm, the fact remains that they did inflict it on you. You are now living with the results of that harm.

The words those people spoke to you are part of the reason you are unable to give yourself the time and patience required to progress in your healing journey. You have taken those words into yourself and believe them to be true. Indeed, you believe them to be your own words and thoughts. Because of this, when you struggle or stumble in your journey, you condemn yourself as "bad" or believe you will never be able to heal.

Finding compassion for yourself and being patient when your journey appears to have stalled will be the most difficult parts of the journey. You will be required to not only continue to work when no progress is made, but you will need to accept that this is part of working toward healing. You will need to accept yourself as one who cannot complete the journey and cannot progress the way you wish.

We do not use the word "cannot" to limit you, but rather to denote an inability that is truth. No human who is on a healing journey will complete it in their current lifetime, for healing is something which transcends incarnation and continues into future lives. When a human does finally reach a point at which they are nearing the end of their journey, they no longer need to incarnate to continue their work. This is the point at which they may choose to serve as spirit guides to those who come after them or may choose a different form of existence that does not require a physical body.

When we say you cannot complete the journey, we do not intend to dissuade you from the work, but merely to remind you of the fact that no human will be fully healed in their current lifetime. Expecting yourself to reach a state of "fully healed" will only result in further anger and hatred toward yourself when you do not reach that point. You can, however, progress. You can grow. And you shall do so if you choose.

Similarly, when we say you cannot progress the way you wish, we do not intend to say that you cannot progress at all. Rather, we are stating that the way you wish to heal is unrealistic for you or for any other human on a healing journey. You have set unreasonable expectations for yourself based upon what you were told by those who harmed you, or perhaps based upon a desire to prove to them that they were wrong.

Setting expectations for yourself is not harmful in and of itself, though we would encourage you to set hopes and desires rather than expectations. The word "expectation" often connotes being obligated to perform the action, or being required to do it. It places a burden upon you in that if you do not meet the expectation, you fear the consequences and therefore condemn yourself. For some, expectations feel like traps. The word leads to the belief that you have no other option but to do what is expected.

However, the words "hope" and "desire" do not carry the same connotation. They are more beneficial words. They carry possibilities rather than requirements. Some of you, in reading the word "expectation," felt heavy and unhappy. Reading the words "hope" and "desire" bring you a feeling of happiness and open you to the realization that you have the power to control what comes next for you.

Therefore, we encourage you to set hopes and desires. We encourage you to hope that you will accomplish certain things in your healing journey but remain open to the possibility that you will not. Some of you will find that releasing the expectation of accomplishment will enable you to accomplish more, for you will no longer feel the pressure and fear that accompanies expectations. You will perceive the possibilities of all that you might accomplish and what you might not, and you will become able to understand that it is acceptable not to meet every goal in the time period you have set.

You have choices. You have options. No harm will come, no punishment will be wrought upon you, if you do not progress in a set amount of time or do not accomplish certain tasks.

As some of you read those words, you are crafting arguments against them. "I don't have a choice about getting better. If I don't get better, I will lose this loved one." "If I can't stop being afraid of authority, I will be unable to hold a job, and I need a job." Perhaps you have even been given ultimatums by others that you must reach a certain point in your journey by a certain time or they will do something you do not want, such as removing themselves from your life.

These beliefs and potential consequences are holding you back from the progress you wish to make. The beliefs and fears are thought patterns created in part through the harm you have experienced. The ultimatums given by others may be their true intention, but your choice need not be determined by them.

That latter statement gives rise to further argument. If someone has stated that if you do not get better they will leave you, how can you choose otherwise? And how can you allow yourself the time you truly need if their ultimatum has a time limit?

Each thing you do in life is a choice. The choice may be made because the alternatives are unpleasant or even harmful, but nonetheless, it is a choice.

This, however, does not mean you choose the actions of other people. As we have discussed, you are not responsible for what others choose to do or say. You are not the one who chose the harm you have experienced. That was the choice of those who inflicted the harm. Although they may have said otherwise, they did choose those actions. Perhaps they knew no other choice to make, but that does not excuse them, nor does it change the fact that they made a choice when they caused harm to you.

When you are unaware that you have the power to choose, at times it may appear as if you have no choice. If the alternatives are unpleasant or harmful, you may believe you have only one option because you wish to choose the option that will have the least negative impact upon you. So often, humans say they have no choice, yet this is not a true statement. They may be unaware of the options or may not wish to deal with the alternatives, but nonetheless, a choice exists to be made.

So it is with your healing journey. You choose whether to embark upon this journey. This is not a choice you are required to make, regardless of what others may say. You may instead choose not to address the issues your experiences have left behind. You may choose to continue with behaviors and patterns you know to be problematic. You may choose to live with the nightmares and fears caused by the rewiring of your brain.

Or you may choose to begin your healing journey. You may choose to seek assistance to determine what you need to do and how best to do it. You may choose to be more mindful of your actions, words, and patterns and work on eradicating those that are problematic.

By stating that you have no choice but to begin a healing journey, you are stating that you have no power or control of your life. You are abdicating responsibility for your life and simply waiting for things to happen on their own or for others to do things for or to you. This is not a beneficial way to live your life, yet any time you claim to have no choice, no matter the circumstances, this is what you are doing.

You will gain greater benefit by stating the truth, that you are choosing to embark on your healing journey. You are choosing to address the alterations and issues caused by trauma. Even if it appears or feels as if you have no choice, in truth, you have the power to make other decisions. By stating that you choose to begin your healing journey, you are connecting with and claiming your inner power and are regaining control of your life. You are acknowledging your responsibilities to yourself and others and recognizing that you are capable of meeting those responsibilities. Does this not sound like a more beneficial way to live?

How you engage and progress in this journey is also a matter of choice. There are a number of ways you may begin and continue to heal. In this, it is even more important to recognize that choices may be made, for some methods of healing will not work for you and may lead to you believing you cannot heal. You have the power to progress in this journey if you find the methods that are most beneficial for you. Even if others who seem to have more knowledge than you state that a given method will work, you may choose not to listen if their method does not feel right for you.

The amount of time this journey will take is not entirely a matter of choice, for the length of the journey is affected by the extent of the harm you have experienced and the extent of the effects that harm left behind. That is not a choice, any more than bleeding when cut by a blade is a choice. Just as physical wounds take varying amounts of time to heal, the mental, emotional, and energetic wounds left by your experiences will heal in lengths of time that cannot be accurately predicted.

In the length of time your healing journey takes, your choice lies in whether or not to accept how long it is. You may choose to honor yourself and your needs by accepting that healing takes time and you are not broken or unable to heal because your journey may last longer than you would like. You may choose to continue to work even when your ego and the voices of your past claim that you will never progress to the point you wish.

There are other choices involved in the healing journey which we will discuss in a later chapter, for they are relevant to a different topic. On the topic of patience with your healing journey, we encourage you to choose to begin, to choose to continue, to choose to accept that no matter how long it takes, you are progressing.

We also encourage you to accept the times of feeling stuck or regressing. That is another choice to make, for you may also choose to be angry with yourself or to give up. Of course, we do not advise those choices, for they will not benefit you. Yet even so, they are choices you may make.

Throughout your life, you have had free will, even though at times it has seemed otherwise. Throughout your life, in a number of contexts, you have had times when progress has slowed or come to a halt or when you have seemed to be going backward. These things have applied in many areas of your life, such as learning to walk and speak, your school studies, perhaps learning the tasks included in your job. They have likely applied in your friendships and relationships and in your parenting if you are one who has children.

In all aspects of life, there is no such thing as a straightforward journey. There are nearly always stops and struggles and regressions along the way. When these have occurred in your life, you may have become angry with yourself and looked down upon yourself. That is a natural response given what others have put upon you through the harm they inflicted. It is possible that even now, reading these words, you are thinking, "Yes, I've done that, why can't I remember to be compassionate with myself, what is wrong with me?" And that, too, is a thought caused by the impressions and patterns others have put upon you.

These impressions and patterns may not entirely disappear. They have become part of the alterations of your brain caused by your experiences. When certain stimuli are presented that remind you of the harm, your brain will respond as if those experiences are currently occurring, and this may include engaging in the patterns created at the time those experiences actually happened.

However, you may choose to learn to recognize when they are arising. You may choose to learn to recognize when you have been triggered into a state in which your brain reacts to past harm as if it were current. You may choose to learn techniques to manage your reactions during those times.

We speak of a healing journey because it is something that will happen over time. There will not be a moment at which you can say "I am now healed." Rather, there will be moments at which you are able to notice your progress, moments at which there is no progress, and moments at which you perceive no progress even though it is occurring. All of these are part of the journey, and you are encouraged to allow the journey to unfold in the way that most benefits you. However long that may take.

Cause No Harm

When an animal is in pain, it lashes out. It will attack any who approach it because the pain has dulled the animal's ability to distinguish threat from ally.

Likewise, when a human is in pain, they may lash out. This is true whether the pain is physical or emotional, and in fact is more likely at times of emotional pain. Humans are taught how to cope with physical pain, and tools exist to alleviate it. The pain of emotions and thoughts over which the human does not have full control is much greater, and fewer tools exist to aid the person in managing it.

Physical pain generally, though not always, has a finite timespan. Barring chronic conditions, a human experiencing physical pain can pinpoint when it began, and they or a physician may be able to pinpoint an approximate time at which it might end.

This is not often the case with emotional pain, particularly pain caused by traumatizing experiences. For some who have experienced this level of harm by others, there is no identifiable starting point. The harm always occurred. There was no respite. This may have been literally true or may be the perception owing to memory deficits created by the trauma, which makes the perception no less true for that person.

There is no pain medication that will touch emotional pain, though some medications do exist that enable one to better manage the pain when it arises. There is no predicting how long the emotional pain will last or whether it will ever completely come to an end.

When one lives with constant emotional pain, one may begin to lash out at others. This may take the form of blaming others for the condition or for not understanding the person's experiences. It may take the form of physically lashing out or of verbally attacking another.

These actions arise from the pain and fear within, but that does not excuse you for acting in this manner. There is no valid excuse for knowingly causing harm or pain to another. Regardless of what you have experienced in the past, it is your responsibility to learn to manage in such a way that no one is harmed.

This includes yourself. Because there are not methods of completely alleviating emotional pain, and the methods of relieving it to any extent may not be effective or available, some turn to what humans term "self-medication." Someone may begin to utilize alcohol or other mind-altering substances to attempt to correct the alterations already existent in the mind due to the trauma. They may not believe these substances will change the rewiring of the brain, but hope the substances will dull the pain.

Use of these substances is not the only form of self-medication in which one who has experienced harm might engage. Some may instead turn to excessive spending, even to the point of being unable to meet financial responsibilities, because shopping takes away their awareness of the emotional anguish. Some may turn to excessive sexual experiences in which they take no joy or pleasure but merely are able to temporarily forget their pain. Some may sleep far beyond the amount of time needed for health so that they do not have to think about anything.

None of these things, used in moderation or in ways that bring joy and pleasure, is inherently harmful. The harm comes from using them to a point of excess for the purpose of alleviating emotional pain. When you seek to eliminate your awareness of the pain rather than seeking to treat and manage it, you are harming yourself.

You may also lash out at yourself. Many who have survived harmful experiences become unable or unwilling to view themselves with kindness and compassion. Rather, they insult themselves or make damaging statements. They condemn themselves for their current state, for harm they may have inflicted upon others knowingly or not, for not being healed, or for a myriad of other reasons. They may even extend this to physically harming themselves.

This does not serve you. It does not remove the pain; in fact, it increases your pain, for you are now inflicting it upon yourself. Even if you have caused harm to others, even if you knew at the time that you were causing harm, condemning and hating yourself for it will not erase what occurred and will not help you progress toward healing. As you work toward your own healing, you will have the responsibility to make apologies and amends to those you harmed, but accepting responsibility is not the same as dwelling upon the occurrences to the extent of self-hatred.

Regardless of what you have done in your life, even if you have caused harm, you do not deserve to be hated. Some whom you have harmed may hate you, and that is their choice to make, for you do not have a right to dictate how another feels about you. You may apologize to them and have that apology rejected. That is also their choice. You may offer to make amends and be met with anger and refusal. That is their choice.

However, you do not deserve to be hated. You do not deserve to consider yourself a "bad person" or believe you deserve to be somehow punished or treated poorly because you have committed actions which caused harm.

This does not mean that your actions were acceptable. They were not. It means merely that just as you are not your experiences, you likewise are not your actions. The actions were unacceptable. The actions may be deserving of hatred. But you, as a whole person, are not.

The actions you have committed likely arose from the pain and fear within you, or from the automatic reactions to perceived threats that come from the altered part of your brain. There were reasons for them, even if those reasons are difficult to determine or were not directly connected to the person whom you harmed.

It is important to remember that a reason is not an excuse. You may find explanations and causes for your actions, but that does not mean the actions were acceptable. The choice to commit those actions may have been unconscious on your part and may have been impacted by automatic reactions, but still, you did on some level make a choice.

Again, this does not mean you are a bad person. It is extremely rare for an entire being to be "bad" or "wrong" or "evil." Rather, there are people who are neither good nor bad, who do and say things that may be judged by those terms. Whether you unconsciously or consciously chose an action that brought harm to another—or to yourself—you are not a bad person. You have simply made incorrect and detrimental choices and committed harmful actions. The judgment is upon the actions, not the person.

This concept may be difficult for some of you to digest or accept, for you have been taught that only "bad people" do "bad things." This is not so. Humans are creatures of balance and choice, and they are not always capable of making choices that are beneficial. Even if one chooses an action they believe will be of benefit, there is a risk of unintentionally causing pain or harm. Not every harmful action is intentional; many are not. Sometimes harm is caused without intention, or "by accident" as some may say, rather than with intent and malice.

This is, in fact, often the case for those who operate from a place of trauma, for your ability to accurately predict the outcome of an action may be impaired. You may take an action you believe will be beneficial only to realize, once the action has been performed, that it was in fact harmful to you or someone else. You may even be unable to recognize the results of that action after they have occurred, or may see that something has happened but be unable to connect it to the action you took.

Inability to perceive cause and effect, inability to accurately judge the impact your actions may have, does not translate to lack of responsibility for those actions. You are responsible for the things you do and say and for the results and consequences thereof, even if you took those actions believing they would be of benefit. You are responsible for the choices you make and the consequences of those choices, even if you were unaware at the time that you were making a choice.

There is a human saying: "Hurt people hurt people." This is often stated to mean that one who is operating out of pain and trauma is likely to cause pain and harm to others, which is truthful. However, some people utilize this phrase to absolve themselves of responsibility for their actions on the basis that they were hurt and therefore "had no choice" but to behave in the manner they did.

There is no excuse for causing harm. No justification or platitude absolves you of responsibility. You may seek the reasons behind your actions, and in fact are encouraged to do so, for this may bring you deeper recognition of the mental and emotional wounds in need of healing within you. You are, however, urged to refrain from using those reasons to justify your actions or attempt to excuse them or deny responsibility for them. Ultimately, you are responsible for what you say and do. You are responsible for any harm you cause, however inadvertently. You are responsible for the effects and impacts your choices have upon others.

Some of you have read the preceding paragraphs and have concluded that you are to blame for what you have done and what transpired as a result. Some of you are falling more deeply into the pit of self-hatred and negation. Some of you, on the other hand, are doubling down, so to speak, on your insistence that what you have done is not your fault because of what others have done to you.

None of those interpretations is correct.

Responsibility, as we have discussed, does not equate to blame or fault. Blame and fault are negative concepts used to negate and invalidate yourself or others. They keep you mired in a pit of hatred and belief that you cannot heal. They serve no useful purpose and are, in fact, the province of ego and likely the result of inaccurate teachings from those you encountered as a child or from those who caused you harm. Being responsible for your actions and their consequences does not mean you are at fault or to blame. It simply means that you chose those actions, and their outcomes are a direct result of your choices.

Actions, once taken, cannot be untaken. When you make a choice, you are only able to change that choice prior to acting upon it. The past has happened, as humans perceive time, and cannot be altered.

This means that when you have committed harmful actions, you cannot change what you have done. You cannot change the harm you have caused. You can, however, change yourself. You have the power to recognize that your actions and choices caused harm and to choose differently in the future. You have the power to apologize and make amends to those who were affected by your action.

Committing a harmful action does not mean you will always be harmful or that you cannot change. In the past, you have committed actions that would have been best left undone, but you can now choose differently. The actions you take going forward can bring benefit and peace instead of harm.

You are not the person you were when those actions were taken. Even if you performed an action only yesterday, still you are not the person you were at that time, for with each moment you exist, you are growing and changing. These changes are within your control if you wish them to be, for you have the power to create who you are and how your life shall be.

Because you are no longer the person who committed those actions, you need not look at yourself with hatred or disgust. You have changed and grown. You have learned that your actions were unacceptable and harmful. At this time, you possess the knowledge and discernment to choose a different course.

Your actions cannot be erased. Regardless of how greatly you have changed in the intervening time, those actions still occurred and still had an impact upon others. Claiming responsibility for those actions is not claiming that you are still the person who committed them, but rather identifying yourself as the person who, at that time, made that choice. This may seem a very faint distinction, but it is a distinction nonetheless and is being made to prove the point that you need not hate yourself as you are now for what you have done, and also to remind you that you can change, for you have changed.

You are also advised against hating the person you were when you chose those actions. That person was part of you, and perhaps still is among the frozen consciousnesses within your mind and energy. Hating the person you once were will have a deleterious effect on the person you are now, for that energy will ripple throughout your system.

Perhaps you are now able, or will become able in the future, to view that past self with compassion and understanding. Not acceptance of their actions, but acceptance of who they were when those actions were committed. Recognition of the roots and reasons behind the behavior.

Recognizing the roots from which harmful choices arise is not the same as excusing those choices. A reason or root is simply what lies beneath the choice. Excusing an action, on the other hand, is using that reason or root to deny responsibility or to attempt to force others to forgive you and accept you. Those are not beneficial courses of action and do not lead to healing for you or for those who may have been harmed by your choices. There is no excuse for causing harm to another, even if you were unaware at the time that you were causing harm.

Similarly, if another has harmed you, there is no excuse. Some of you attempt to excuse those who caused harm to you because of their pasts or their lack of understanding. These things may have been the roots of their behavior, but they are not excuses. When you attempt to excuse the behavior of one who has caused harm to you, you are in fact furthering that harm, for you are negating your own experiences by prioritizing theirs.

You are on a healing journey, and that journey does not occur without bumps in the road, as it were. There will be difficult times. There will be times when you experience fears and flashbacks and are unable to separate yourself from them. There will be times when you question your worth, your ability to heal, and perhaps even your existence.

At these times, you may lash out at those around you, particularly those who love you, for the parts of you wounded by your past perceive those people as "safe." Much as a toddler will behave more appropriately in an educational setting such as daycare than at home because they perceive their parents as safer people than their teachers, one who is living with and healing from trauma may act less acceptably around the very people who care the most for them.

It likely does not need to be stated that lashing out at anyone, particularly those who are closest to you, is not acceptable. We are not judging you by this statement, but rather reminding you that there are certain behaviors humans deem acceptable, and lashing out is not one of them. Although in the moment verbally attacking another or responding in other harmful ways may feel effective in relieving your pain and fear, that choice will ultimately result in further hatred of yourself for harming one who loves you.

As a vital part of your healing journey, you are encouraged to find ways to manage your emotions and reactions that are not harmful to you or any other. There are management strategies and techniques a therapist may teach you should you choose to engage in therapy, as we also encourage you to do, for a book dictated by two beings formed of pure energy cannot substitute for consistent support and aid from a licensed human professional. We offer these words and any suggestions herein in solely a supportive and supplemental way.

The seemingly simple task of breathing deeply and counting to a specific number may be sufficient for you to de-escalate from the state at which you might cause harm. However, this technique only appears simple when you are in a calm state. When you are already escalating to a point of emotional overload or struggle, you may be unable to remember to utilize this technique. For some, a visual reminder is beneficial so that they can see, when they are in a heightened emotional state, that they have techniques which may aid them.

For some, having a person to whom you can turn for calm support may be of benefit. It is important to ensure that you will use this person as a support rather than as what you might term a "verbal punching bag." River has found it beneficial to sit, at calm times, with their support person and explain what they will need at times of emotional escalation or flashbacks. By doing this, they have ensured that their person will know how to assist them at times when River may be unable to speak to tell the person what is needed. They have also ensured that they will not lash out at that person, because they are aware that the person is there to help and knows what to do, and they are therefore not frightened when the person approaches them.

There are other strategies which work for others at times of emotional escalation. Any nonharmful strategy that assists you in de-escalating and managing your emotions and reactions is of benefit, and as stated, a therapist or other professional is likely to be able to help you determine what will work for you and learn how to implement it. We shall not include a full list here, for what works for one does not work for all, and we are not endeavoring to provide therapy for those who read these words.

Whatever strategies you use, and however you turn to others for help, it is imperative that you manage yourself in ways that cause no harm. Harming yourself or others only serves to further the harm that has already been caused to you.

Experiencing trauma or living with mental illnesses is not justification for behaving in harmful ways. While these things may explain the harmful behavior, they do not excuse it and should not be used to do so. No matter what your experiences have been in the past or where you are in your healing journey, you do have the power to learn to navigate your life in such a way that others as well as yourself experience no negative impacts. You are encouraged to exercise this power.

You Are Not Alone

Some of you view the healing journey as an overwhelmingly complex process. Some of you question whether it is within your capabilities. Some of you believe that even if you turn to your loved ones and friends for support, they will deny it.

Some of you believe you have no loved ones or friends, and indeed, for some this may even be true.

As you consider, begin, and progress in your healing journey, it is our hope that you will remember that you are not alone, even when it appears otherwise. There are other humans who have been through experiences that have left them with trauma. You are not the only one. This is not said to minimize you but rather to empower you, for one of the things that dulls the power of a survivor is the belief that no one else has ever had similar experiences.

There are those who are further along in their healing journeys than you, who may be able and willing to take your hand, as it were, and assist you on your path. It may be difficult to find these people, and you may be unwilling to reach out your hand for them to take, but they are there.

There are those who are less far along on their journeys than you. These people may be unable to assist you in overt ways, but perhaps you will be the one to take their hands and assist them, and perhaps providing this assistance to others will benefit you. When you help another, it may remind you that you are not alone and also that you are valuable and knowledgeable despite what those who harmed you may have said.

There are practitioners who may or may not have experienced traumatizing events themselves but have taken the time to learn about and understand trauma and its effects. These practitioners know how trauma might prevent someone from accessing their services or from perceiving things the way someone who has not experienced trauma would. They have learned how to adjust their practices and ways of presenting things so that a survivor of harmful experiences can benefit and feels supported and heard.

There may be those who love or care for you and want you to be well. Who want you to make progress and understand that this will be a journey in which you will be engaged for the rest of your life. They may not fully comprehend your experiences or what trauma is and does, but they understand *you* and wish to support you in your progression toward healing.

There are licensed professionals of various sorts who are trained in working with those who have experienced trauma. They have studied and learned, and they know techniques and strategies to help you learn to manage where you are while also supporting you as you progress and grow. There are different types of professionals, and each one is an individual with whom you may or may not align, so you are encouraged to continue to seek if necessary rather than settling for the first one you encounter if they do not seem to be someone with whom you can work.

Finally, there are your guides. If you have chosen to read this book, you may already have formed a conscious connection with your guides. Even if you have not, they are with you and hear and see you though you cannot yet hear them or knowingly receive their guidance. They love you unconditionally, for conditional love is not something these beings experience.

Many people struggle to ask for help and support. This can be particularly true for those who have experienced abuse and other trauma, as you may have been taught that no one would help you if you asked or that requesting support is a sign of weakness. Even if you have now recognized on an intellectual level that the latter is not true, and even if you have received help when you have asked, on a deeper level you may still believe these things.

You do not exist in a vacuum. Although you may isolate yourself from other humans, you are not entirely isolated. You know that others are around you and that your actions may impact them as theirs may impact you. Perhaps they have even stated to you that they wish to help and support you. Yet you hesitate to make your needs known.

Your current state was not created by you alone. The trauma and difficulties with which you live were not caused by you, but by others through their harmful actions. Why, then, would you expect to heal alone? If others caused the harm, why do you believe you should not require help from others to progress in healing?

Yet asking for help can be one of the most difficult and even frightening aspects of the healing journey. During the times when you experienced harm, you may have reached out for help only to be rejected, blamed, or disbelieved. The harm may therefore have continued and even may have become worse if the person causing the harm was made aware that you had sought assistance.

Of course experiences such as those would leave you highly reluctant to attempt to obtain help in the future. That is understandable, for your choices and responses are shaped by experience. When experience demonstrates that you cannot ask for help, you learn not to ask.

However, the healing journey is not one to undertake alone. As you begin, you will require guidance and support in determining the steps to take. As you progress, you may encounter deeper wounds and suppressed memories and will need support and perhaps professional assistance to process and work through them. Even if you choose to refrain from seeking professional help, the support and compassion of those close to you will benefit you on this path.

If you are already consciously working with your guides, you may hesitate to ask for their support and assistance out of fear of asking too much or that they may consider you unworthy of working with them if they learn the "truth" about you. This fear, also, is understandable but unwarranted.

We work with you to provide you with love and compassion as you grow and progress. This is unconditional on our part. We love you no less if we learn of your struggles, and indeed, having been with you since your birth, your guides almost certainly already know what you have experienced. We have seen your difficulties in managing the reactions created by trauma. If you have lashed out at others or harmed others, intentionally or not, your guides have seen it. And yet they love you regardless, for the beings who act as guides do not place conditions upon our love, compassion, and support.

You may have read the previous paragraph with skepticism and may even feel anger at those words, for the concept of truly unconditional love is foreign to you. You view it with suspicion and disbelief. No human in your life has granted you unconditional love, or at least none that you have been able to accept, so how could beings such as ourselves give this to you?

It is not in our nature to place conditions upon those things we feel or offer to you. For your guides, the idea of conditional love is as foreign as the concept of unconditional love is for you. There is no explanation for this that can easily be translated into human words, for it is not something meant to be explained. It simply is so.

Your guides are with you to support you in your life journey, of which your healing journey is part. This support takes whatever form you need, but we must have your consent to provide it or we will violate your free will. The violation of free will is something no guide will commit, for it is counter to our purpose. When you ask why you were harmed even though your guides were present, this is why. They could not intervene without violating free will unless you asked for their aid, and if, at the time, you were unaware they were there, you could not ask.

Because of free will, as much as we wish to support and assist you in your healing journey, we cannot do so unless you ask. But once you ask, your guides will be pleased to provide what you need. There is no such thing as asking too much from us, for we are with you to benefit you in whatever ways you wish or require. At times you might ask something from your guides that they are unable to provide, but they will simply state that this is so without any judgment of the fact that you have asked or of you for having asked.

We therefore encourage you to ask your guides for assistance. Even if you do not have a conscious connection with them at this time, you know they are there. They do not require your conscious awareness of them to help you, nor is that level of awareness necessary for you to request their aid. You may say or think something as simple as, "Please help me," and your guides will respond, though you may be unaware that what transpires is actually their assistance.

Amongst humans, truly unconditional love and support is rare, for it is human nature to place some conditions upon nearly everything. This is not wrong; it is simply so. However, for some of you, the conditions you believe others have placed upon their love for you do not exist. They are a creation of your own mind, your own fears, and are not reality. You fear that if certain people find out "who you really are," as you may phrase it, you will lose their love and support.

This is, for many, not the case. All humans have times of struggle and of needing support from others. This is not something exclusive to you or even to all survivors of trauma. Just as it is human nature to place conditions upon things, it is also human nature to have times of difficulty and times of needing aid from others to overcome those difficulties.

Those who care for you are unlikely to turn away if they learn that you are struggling. Indeed, they may already be aware of your struggles and are waiting for you to ask for their help or tell them how best to support you. They might not step in to assist you unless you ask because they may not know what you need from them or might not wish to imply that you are incapable by presuming to do things for you. Or, similarly to your guides, they might not intervene until asked because they wish to honor your autonomy and free will.

However, when you are open with them about your difficulties and your needs, for the most part they will come to your aid. They will support you. Even if they are unable to do what you need done, they will continue to love you and be there for you. Most of them will not think less of you for speaking out about the effects trauma is having upon you and your need for assistance in managing those effects.

It is, of course, possible that some will turn away if you speak the truth about your struggles and needs. If this occurs, we encourage you to understand that it is not because of you, but because of their own fears and struggles. In these instances, you will feel rejected or abandoned, and for some of you this may be upsetting or triggering. But again we say, if people turn from you when you seek help and support, it is not because of you. It is because of something within them, something which causes them to fear. Perhaps even something that has arisen because of their own harmful experiences that they have chosen to deny or ignore.

Many of you have been taught or have come to believe that seeking help is a sign of weakness. You fear being seen as weak and vulnerable, because being seen as such has been a root of the harm you have experienced. We understand why you believe this way, but we wish you to know that it is an incorrect thought pattern and one which is holding you back in your healing journey.

Seeking help is more a sign of strength than attempting to manage everything in isolation. Pretending nothing is wrong or insisting you can do it all yourself is not strength, for you are being dishonest with yourself and others. You are hiding out of fear, and you are negating the parts of you that need and crave support and human connection. This does not make you strong.

In fact, it weakens you further, for you come to believe that your choice to ignore your struggles and refuse any aid is due to other people rather than a conscious decision on your part. You blame those who harmed you for "making you this way" and may even place blame upon those in your life now for not somehow being able to tell that you need help even as you deny this need. You come to resent that you must struggle alone and to further distrust others, despite the choice of refusing to seek help being entirely your choice.

By contrast, seeking help is a sign of strength, for you are overcoming your fear and ego in order to better heal and support the parts of you that require aid. You may still be afraid of the reactions of others, and this, as all emotions, is valid. We do not tell you not to fear seeking help, only that you are powerful enough to seek help despite the fear. Conquering such fears takes immense strength. Indeed, the fact that you have survived and are now reading these words indicates precisely how much strength you have, for you have chosen to remain alive and are choosing to embark or continue on your healing journey despite the obstacles with which you have been presented.

Reaching out to others for assistance and support is further demonstration of this strength, for you are doing so despite the fears and ingrained beliefs left by your past experiences. You are showing trust in others even though in the past you have been shown that you cannot trust. You are expressing, whether with full awareness or not, the belief that you deserve to progress in healing and that you are able to take this journey.

Recognizing that you cannot do everything on your own is not weak. It takes strength to acknowledge that you require aid. It takes strength to say, "I've done all I can without support, so please support me now." It takes strength to come out of the shadows with your experiences and their effects and speak of them to others.

This strength will not go unnoticed. When you reach out for help, you show others they can do the same. You offer opportunities for others to heal as well as for those you approach to help you on your healing journey. This need not be your reason for reaching out. Indeed, we advise against reaching out for support so that you may benefit others, for at this time in your healing journey, it is most advisable to be your own primary focus. But know that as you bring benefit to yourself for choosing to seek aid, you will also benefit others.

You are not alone in this journey. You have never been truly alone, although at times you have felt as if you were. We encourage you to remember this and to make use of the help and support available to you, for even the simple act of saying, "I need help" brings you further in your journey to heal from your past.

Shame Is a Wasted Emotion

Many of you have been taught to feel shame. Because you were blamed for the experiences which harmed you and for the actions of the people who caused the harm, you have learned to be ashamed of your actions and indeed of your very existence.

Shame is a wasted emotion, for it is one of the ultimate falsehoods.

Shame is the acceptance of fault. It is the belief that you are unworthy and that you are flawed and therefore deserving of pain. It is turning hatred and blame upon oneself and taking responsibility for things for which you are not responsible.

To feel shame is to accept the lies of others that you are undeserving. That you chose to be harmed because of some innate quality that somehow renders you "bad." To feel shame is to internalize these lies and tell them to yourself.

When you have experienced harm from others, and particularly when that harm has sexual components, you are taught that you should feel shame. You are taught also that certain emotions and reactions are cause for shame. Therefore, when you consider what you have experienced and how you feel about it, you feel shame over any other emotion, for you have learned that the other emotions are invalid.

Beloveds, we tell you that you have no need for shame, for shame is an illusion. As we have stated, you do not cause the actions of other people and therefore did not cause them to harm you. Being the recipient of harm is not something of which to be ashamed, for this was no action or choice on your part. There is no fault or blame and so there is no reason to feel shame or self-hatred.

However, we know that simply reading those words will not eliminate the shame you feel, for that feeling comes from a deeper part of you than can be reached by logic and words printed upon a page. Shame is a falsehood but is also a deep wound, one which must be addressed and treated before you can fully involve yourself in your healing journey.

Others have convinced you to be ashamed of what you have experienced because they are uncomfortable. Hearing what has transpired in your life reminds them that something similar could occur, or perhaps has already occurred, in theirs. They enforce shame upon you in order to separate themselves from you. If you have done something of which to be ashamed, that means they are safe from harm so long as they do not do what you have done. Or so they believe.

Of course, that is not the case at all. You have done nothing for which you deserve blame or shame. You have done nothing to cause the harm you have experienced. There is no course of action you have taken that renders you responsible for the choices others have made, and therefore there is no choice those who attempt to shame you could make that would render them completely safe.

That is frightening for them to hear, for they wish and perhaps even need to believe that only "certain people" experience harm. That only incorrect actions and choices will result in abuse or attack. They need to believe they have the ability to control that which cannot be controlled or to exert their control over those who might intend harm.

We do not judge them for these beliefs, for it is human nature to attempt to make sense of the inexplicable. Throughout history, and even now in the era in which we convey these words, humans create explanations and theories in an effort to bring reason to the unreasonable. If they can explain and find reasons for certain occurrences, they believe they can protect themselves from similar events.

However, although it is not in our nature to judge, we do acknowledge and state that their refusal to accept that they cannot control everything that occurs in their lives causes further damage to those who have already experienced great harm. Their insistence that one who has been abused is to blame for the abuse only reinforces what the one who inflicted the abuse stated. The forcing of shame upon those who have been harmed only deepens the wounds.

Shame is not only something enforced upon you by others. It is something which becomes internalized, so that you come to believe that you are, in fact, responsible for what has been done to you. You become one of those who inflicts harm upon you by accepting the weight of false beliefs about who is truly responsible for causing harm.

Additionally, shame breeds silence. When you feel shame about your experiences or about the emotions and effects within you as a result of those experiences, you do not speak of them lest others shame you as well. You remain silent about what has occurred. You suppress or even entirely deny the existence of difficult emotions and your reactions to them. You place a façade between yourself and the world so that no one else will know the truth and therefore no one else will insist that you must be ashamed.

Silence about your experiences will not lead to healing. Denial of the existence of painful memories or difficult emotions does not enable you to effectively address and manage them. You do yourself a vast disservice by allowing shame to silence you.

Indeed, you do a disservice to many, including yourself, for when someone speaks out about their experiences and acknowledges their emotions and pain, it demonstrates to others who have been harmed that they can do the same. That they may come out of hiding and speak of what has occurred and the effects those experiences have left. By refuting and refusing shame and speaking openly, you are contributing to the healing journeys of others as well as your own.

It is easy for us to say you may cease feeling shame, but we do not intend to minimize the difficulty of actually doing so. For some of you, shame began very early in your life and was constantly reinforced. This will take time to overcome. It is unreasonable to expect that you can simply choose not to feel shame and have those feelings cease.

But the release of shame is something toward which you may choose to work. With each moment that you consider your past experiences without a sense of shame and without considering yourself at fault, you make immense progress and demonstrate to others that they may do the same.

Just as you are not alone in your healing journey, you are not alone in the struggles. You are not healing in a vacuum but rather as part of a grand Whole. The progress you make in your own healing journey ripples outward.

Those others who have committed harm see that you are stronger than they. This may cause them to reconsider actions they commit against those they believe to be weak. Some will come to understand and recognize the harm their actions have brought and will cease to commit those actions, for while causing harm is a choice, for some it is a choice made on an unconscious level based upon the harm they themselves have experienced. When these people see that they have caused harm, they will take steps to change their behavior and perhaps make amends to those they have harmed.

More importantly, those who have experienced harm will see your healing journey. Some will reject the possibility for themselves and will even condemn you for having the audacity to speak about your experiences. This response comes from the wounded parts of them, from the parts that believe they must not speak of what has occurred. It is not about you, but rather about their anger and frustration in seeing someone else receive support while they themselves fear even asking.

Perhaps some of them, in seeing that you do not receive further harm from speaking out and in fact receive help and support, might change their way of thinking. They might take the risk of speaking about their own experiences, thereby receiving the help and support they need. At the very least, they might accept that some people will speak out about harmful experiences and that this is not "weakness" or "whining."

Those who believe that in general there is no harm or weakness in speaking out may believe that for them personally, there would be harm. Some of them can see that for others, there is no shame in having been recipients of harm and abuse, but are unable to apply that belief to themselves. When you speak openly of having experienced harm, these people might recognize themselves in your story and may begin to believe that if you were not at fault, perhaps they were not either.

In reading those words, some of you are concluding that you must take the risk of speaking out in order to help others. This is not our intention. What you do for others may be highly beneficial, but it must not be the sole reason for you to seek healing and speak of what has transpired in your life. The release of shame and acceptance of your Self as whole and unsullied must be on an individual basis, something done for yourself rather than for others. If you choose healing solely for the benefit of others, you are continuing a pattern you formed during the time of trauma, when you began acting in ways you hoped would minimize the harm.

Therefore, we strongly encourage you to seek healing first for your own benefit. We encourage you to speak out because of the positive effects it may have upon you. We invite you to come out of hiding so that you may perceive and experience yourself as a full being, not merely as the sum of abuse and harm.

We speak of the beneficial effect your choices may have upon others not so that you will take this as the sole or primary reason you should progress and work toward healing, but rather to remind you that just as the effects of harm are not confined to only one or two people, neither are the effects of healing. You are healing for yourself, but that choice will have a beneficial impact upon those who see the choice and the actions you take as a result.

Shame is something inflicted upon humans by other humans for many reasons. When you choose to refute that shame and refuse to accept blame for the harm you have experienced, you will begin to recognize that you need not feel shame about anything. Humans are taught to feel shame for going against societal norms created by other humans, albeit sometimes in the name of serving a higher power. The Ultimate Creator does not judge you; the belief that it does is a belief created by humans.

Whether we speak of abuse and harm, or of engaging in sexual activities society deems "wrong" or "too much," or of wearing clothing some people consider inappropriate, shame is endemic in your society, and it only serves to cause further harm. It provides the shadows in which abuse occurs. It covers those who inflict harm while shredding those who receive the harm. It creates a blanket of silence under which those who live with trauma are forced to believe they caused it and therefore are alone and unworthy of support or love.

It is not for any individual human to single-handedly conquer shame and bring to light the harm humans do to one another. But with each individual who speaks out, with each one who shines a light into the darkness of shame and hatred, changes occur, and these changes ripple outward to affect more and more beings.

As you progress on your own healing journey and choose to speak out despite fear and shame, you are benefiting yourself. You are bringing to light the core Self within and allowing that Self to have a full life rather than to remain hidden under a pile of fears and harm. You are creating a life in which you receive and accept the love and support of which you are abundantly worthy.

But you also provide healing for others. You shine a light which acts as a beacon to those in need of support on their healing journeys. You demonstrate that harm caused is the sole responsibility of the one who causes it, not the one who receives it.

You allow others to reconnect with their core Selves as they recognize that they were never to blame for their experiences and that they, too, are abundantly worthy of love, support, and healing.

If you have never understood how valuable and important you are in the Universe, it is our hope that you now understand. It is our hope that you have now begun to see yourself as you truly are rather than as the accumulation of others' actions and hatred.

It is our hope that you will choose to begin if you have not already done so, for you are needed and wanted. More, you are loved, and you deserve to feel that love for yourself and allow yourself the fullness of its experience.

The Power to Choose

As you have read the preceding pages, some of you have had visceral reactions to our words. Perhaps mixed reactions, partially hope and partially anger. You both believe and disbelieve what you have read, for the rational part of your mind recognizes truth but the fragmented consciousnesses and trauma-impacted parts of your mind reject truth.

You have reached a point in your life at which you have the power to choose. You may choose whether to pursue healing. Whether to believe what is said in this book. Whether to make changes in your life or continue as you have been going.

What we have stated does not resonate for some of you. You feel it to be false or to be true for some but not yourself. That is valid. You need not take our words as fact solely because we are beings of light and possess high energetic vibration. Among the choices within your power is the choice to accept or reject guidance and information that is offered to you.

As stated previously, your healing journey is entirely your own to be made and created in whatever way you believe will best serve you. You may choose to ignore those who tell you otherwise. If someone claims to understand your needs and journey better than you do yourself, you may choose to discount their words, for no one can know you better than you know yourself. However, you may also choose to listen to them.

You may have chosen this book out of the belief that it would give you all of the answers you seek. We cannot give you all of the answers, for there are some things unknown even to us. And some of what we do know cannot be shared with you at this time due to the risk of interfering with your free will.

The most vital thing for you to remember is that you hold more answers than you realize. Many of the questions you have about your experiences and your journey can be answered with knowledge you yourself carry. However, you have learned to doubt your own knowledge and understanding, and so you seek others to provide answers for you or confirm what you already know rather than trusting the knowledge.

This is another choice you may make: whether to continue seeking answers from others or reconnect with the part of you that already knows the answers. Some of you are frightened at the prospect of trusting yourself, or you believe we are telling you that you are on your own. That is not our intention. You are never truly alone, nor will your guides leave you to struggle without guidance and support.

However, when you come to rely on others more than you are willing to rely upon yourself, it may become an impediment to your healing. If you are unable or unwilling to seek answers within, if you are unable to trust yourself, you will continue to be opposed on your journey. That opposition does not come from external sources or from your past experiences, but from the division between your rational mind and your trauma-impacted thoughts and patterns.

Remember that beneath everything you have experienced lies your core Self. This Self is not divided as your conscious mind is. The core Self holds the knowledge and answers you seek. It trusts even when consciously you do not.

You may choose to reconnect with that Self at this time. This is a process for which you may desire or need support, for it is an undertaking which may lead to buried memories rising to the surface and to cognitive dissonance as you begin to realize some of the beliefs you have formed through your experiences are, in fact, false. If you choose to reconnect with your core Self, you may of course do so with no support, but we would advise you to, at the very least, request aid from your guides.

There are also other humans who may be able to assist you in the process should you choose to ask. Those who practice a form of energy healing may be able to restore the energetic connections and energy flow broken by the harm inflicted on you. A channel may be able to work with their own guides, and through them with your guides, to support the connection to Self on a more concrete level.

Living through traumatic experiences and living with the effects of trauma is not cause for shame or hiding. Your belief that you must keep these things to yourself is part of what has held you back in your journey thus far. Whether your desire to hide and pretend all is well was spawned from the words and actions of those who harmed you or from ideas such as the belief that you must only think positively or must forgive anyone regardless of what they have done, you have that desire.

But all is not well, or you would not be reading these words. Deep within, you know there is more work to be done on your journey. You know that as much as you wish you were unaffected by your experiences, those effects are there.

This does not mean you are damaged or broken. Those are fallacious beliefs that also serve to hold you back, for if you are "broken," surely it is not your responsibility to repair yourself, or so part of you may believe. You are not nor have you ever been broken, although you may have felt that way at times. Rather, you are in the process of healing, and this is a process that takes time and may have setbacks.

If you have ever sustained a severe injury or undergone major surgery, you have gone through a recovery process which may have taken longer than you would have liked. This process may have necessitated additional medical care and may have caused you to be unable to do certain things or to need to do them in ways other than that to which you were previously accustomed. You may have needed more rest than before. At times, your recovery may have felt as if it had stalled. You may even have felt as if the injury or the surgical incision had gotten worse or was more painful.

This is the case also with mental and emotional wounds. Healing is a process that will take time. It cannot be rushed, nor is attempting to rush the process a wise choice to make, though of course as with everything it is a choice available to you. However, attempting to force your healing to occur more rapidly may result in further wounds and in more regression and stagnation. Allowing yourself to take the journey in the time that works best for you is the most beneficial choice, even though it may lead to frustration on your part.

Speaking about your experiences is also a choice. For some of you, choosing to speak will aid you on your journey. You will feel less alone when others listen to you and perhaps tell you they have also had traumatic experiences. The act of cutting the bonds of secrecy and shame and openly verbalizing what has occurred in your life can be a way of reconnecting with your inner power. Speaking out can also bring benefit to others.

However, for some of you, speaking too openly can lead to repercussions from external sources or within yourself. Those who are associated with the person or people who harmed you may become angry when they learn that you have spoken about what has been done. If you are still in a position where you are threatened by these people and are not in a safe place, we encourage you to seek safety and to take the steps needed to protect yourself, including remaining silent about your experiences for the time being if necessary.

Discussing your experiences, for some of you, can also lead to mentally reliving them in vivid detail, which causes the systems affected by trauma to activate. You then react to your experiences as if they were occurring in the present moment. You may struggle to process even things which you previously had processed. If you know that talking about what has been done to you might cause this sort of reaction, you do not need to speak. Perhaps you may write in a private journal about the experiences, or talk about them only to a professional who is assisting you. Or you may choose not to express them in any way, spoken or written.

Whatever you do in your healing journey is a choice. There is no circumstance in which choice is taken away from you, although there are situations in which one or more of the options is not safe for you or is otherwise unviable. Even when it appears as if you have no choice, as if there is only one possible course of action, we encourage you to remember that you are making a choice. You are choosing to act in the way that brings you the least harm or consequence. You may see it as having no other option, but remembering that that is not the case will benefit you, for it will help you remember and reconnect with your inner power.

Any choice is best made after consideration of the options and potential outcomes. For some who live with the effects of trauma, considering cause and effect is difficult. However, it is beneficial to at least try and perhaps to discuss the situation with someone else who can help you recognize the potential outcomes of the given choices and why those outcomes are possible. Consciously choosing the path you take necessitates being conscious of all aspects of the choice. Otherwise you are continuing to live an unconscious life in which things simply happen with no direction from you. You have already seen that this sort of life does not benefit you, for some of you have been living unconsciously for a long while out of fear of embracing your inner power or the belief that you have no power.

Conscious creation is a term often tossed about by those who utilize it to negate and invalidate those who have experienced harm. These people use the concept to claim that humans create everything that occurs in their lives whether harmful or beneficial, and extend this to placing responsibility or even blame upon those who have been harmed for having had those experiences, similarly to the way they interpret and regurgitate the so-called Law of Attraction.

As we have discussed, this is not, in fact, the meaning of the concept. Conscious creation means that you have the power to choose. It means that you have the ability to make decisions and take courses of action that lead you toward creating the most beneficial life available to you. It does not mean you have created everything in your life thus far, nor that if someone causes you harm it is your creation. It simply means becoming aware of your inner power and making the conscious decision to embrace and use it.

The key, of course, is being conscious. Some humans find it very difficult to consider and weigh their options. They would prefer to simply act and "get it over with" or even to have someone else tell them what to do or take action on their behalf. In order to consciously create your life, it is necessary to release these patterns and learn to consider the possibilities. You will need to become comfortable with your own thoughts and with being patient when it comes to taking action. You will need to connect with yourself and your Self even if that feels uncomfortable or frightening. Otherwise you are continuing to live unconsciously and are therefore unable to embrace your power or create benefit for yourself.

Few of the choices that lie before you are easy. The very prospect of embarking and progressing on a healing journey is fraught with difficulty and even pain. However, it is not the same kind of pain that others have inflicted upon you. Rather, it is the emotional and energetic equivalent of what humans call "growing pains." It may hurt. You may struggle.

Perhaps some of the people in your life will turn away from you, not because of who you are but because they are unwilling to accept that you wish to change. This is not a reflection on you but rather is a result of their fears of their own healing journeys and their fear that you will somehow become superior to them or will no longer want or need them in your life. And indeed, you may not wish them to remain in your life as you progress. Be mindful of those who are currently in your life who do not wish the best for you, and be prepared to sever ties with them if necessary so that you may continue to heal.

The choice to end contact and connection with someone, particularly a family member or someone who has been part of your life for many years, is also a difficult one. Many humans are taught that family bonds are inviolable and must be maintained at any cost—including the cost of your own mental and physical well-being. Clearly this maintaining of harmful connections does not serve you, nor does it lend itself to your healing journey. However, many people are held back in their journeys by the belief that they must not cut ties with family members.

We wish you to know that as long as you do so in a nonharmful manner, you may sever these ties, and indeed may need to if you are to truly progress in your journey. If someone with whom you attempt to maintain ties is one of those who harmed you, it is obvious that keeping in contact with that person is not beneficial to your healing. Yet some of you insist that you must keep ties with them regardless because they are family or "they did not mean to."

You know this to be untrue; perhaps their goal was not to cause harm, but they still made the choices that brought harm to you. They may currently be making choices that are equally harmful to you or may be choosing not to acknowledge or admit to their past actions and the effects upon you. Regardless of who they are or what their role has been in your life, if they have made choices that have harmed you and refuse to accept responsibility for those choices, you are not required to allow them a place in your life going forward. And allowing them a place may prevent you from progressing in your healing journey.

No bond between humans, whether a bond of blood or of other factors, requires you to continue allowing someone to be part of your life. The human insistence that "family is forever" or that you must accept harmful behavior from a family member solely because of their blood relationship to you is a fallacy, one which brings ongoing harm and trauma not only to an individual but often to the family as a whole, or even to children who are born into the family and are repeatedly exposed to someone who has already demonstrated that they do not hesitate to bring harm to a child.

In part, your healing journey necessitates your conscious awareness of the impact people have in one another's lives. Not only the impact others have had upon you or the impact you have had upon them, but also the impact that those who have caused harm to you may be having upon others. By removing those people from your life, you are not only protecting yourself but may also protect others for whom you are responsible, such as your children. You are also demonstrating that no one is required to permit anyone else a place in their life, and that it is not only allowable but preferable to cut ties with someone who knowingly causes harm. This demonstration may give others the courage to cut ties with those who have harmed them.

Again, it is not your responsibility to bring healing to others. It is undesirable to take action solely because of the benefit others may gain. We speak of the beneficial effect your actions may have upon others to remind you that you do not exist in isolation and also to remind you of your worth and value in the Universe.

Things that you do, choices that you make, have repercussions of which you may never be aware, whether positive or negative. Therefore, we encourage you to take action that benefits you and may also benefit others, for in addition to progressing in your own journey, you may be the one who causes another survivor to embark on their journey. You may be the reason they believe they can work toward healing—and the reason they believe they deserve to do so.

In any process, someone must take the first step. In the process of healing from past harm, the one who has received the harm will need to take their own steps, but the first step may not be theirs. Rather, it may be a step taken by another and witnessed by the one who wishes to heal. The steps you take will be seen and may show others that they, too, may take steps.

We encourage you to choose the path that best serves you in your healing journey, provided that path brings no harm to you or any other. At times you may wish harm upon those who have harmed you or may imagine them receiving harm. These thoughts, so long as they do not spur you to action, are not damaging in and of themselves, and you need not condemn yourself for them. However, it is wisest for you to acknowledge and dismiss these thoughts when they arise rather than dwelling upon them or allowing them to influence your choices. Your goal in this journey is not to retaliate against those who harmed you, but rather to rise above that harm and create your most beneficial life.

Similarly, as you work and progress in this journey, you may experience emotions such as anger, fear, and even hatred. Hatred is an emotion to be released, for it negates others and brings damage to you energetically and emotionally. Anger and fear, on the other hand, are simply human emotions, neither beneficial nor harmful in and of themselves. If you condemn yourself for feeling these emotions or attempt to deny or bury them, you will block yourself on your journey.

Humans do not choose the emotions they feel; emotions arise as automatic responses to certain stimuli. You do, however, choose how to react or respond to the emotions. When it comes to emotions humans label as negative, we encourage you to respond by allowing the emotions to exist and acknowledging the aspects of yourself from which they arise while taking steps to ensure that you do not bring harm to yourself or any other through your expression of the emotions.

Choosing to accept yourself as human will be one of the most beneficial things you can do during this journey. Some of you have concluded that you are somehow less than human because this is what you were told and shown during the time of harm. Some of you believe that concepts which apply to all other humans, such as the idea that all emotions are valid, do not apply to you.

You are human. Regardless of your energetic origins, for some of you have not originated in your current world, in this lifetime and timeframe, you are human. If humans are allowed to feel emotions, you are allowed to as well. If humans deserve to live free from harm, so do you. If you would recognize your experiences as abusive if someone else told you those were their experiences, the experiences were abusive for you as well.

Of course you are different from all other humans, but only insofar as each human is different from all others. Each human is unique. However, all are still human.

Being human includes making errors at times or choosing courses of action that are detrimental or harmful. This is nothing for which to condemn yourself or feel shame. We encourage you to choose to recognize that you have made these errors and choices, but also to choose to be compassionate with yourself while not repeating those errors. You may judge the action without judging yourself as a being.

Throughout your journey toward healing, you will encounter numerous choices and decisions. Some of these will be difficult for you because you do not know which course is the most ideal or you fear making the wrong choice. At times, your choices will prove to be incorrect, but this is not something to fear. Very few courses of action exist that cannot be undone, repaired, or for which you cannot at least apologize and make amends. If you choose incorrectly, once you have realized it, you may take steps to correct your course or even begin anew.

Above all, the choice you will be asked to make over and over again is the choice to accept yourself as an incredible being who deserves to be well and be loved. Each time you make this choice, even against the voices in your mind speaking cruelty or the external voices arguing with your desire to heal, you will progress further. Each time you choose yourself, you are closer to healing.

How, then, will you choose?

A Closing Message from Shiva and Pietkela

As we have worked in collaboration throughout this project, we have chosen to jointly offer our closing message rather than doing so separately.

In your world, so many are wounded and harmed by others. This is an unfortunate fact of the human existence. It is, however, a fact which is beginning, slowly and almost imperceptibly, to change.

With each successive generation, humans gain more and more understanding of the effects events and experiences may have upon the mind, body, and energy system. They find connection with others who have experienced harm and compare notes, as it were, thereby learning that not only are they not alone, but their experiences and the effects thereof are valid. They are not imagining things or "seeking attention." They are living a life impacted, perhaps repeatedly, by the damaging choices of others.

As more is understood of these effects, and as more survivors band together to speak out, a shift occurs. Each time even one individual chooses to say, "This harmed me and I shall not inflict that harm upon others," the human world moves closer to broader healing and to a form in which humans do not choose to harm one another.

Some of you have already begun to move forward in this process. You have chosen to refrain from treating your children as your parents or other caregivers treated you. You have chosen to seek professional assistance in crafting a life in which you progress toward healing while ensuring that you do not cause anyone else to need to heal.

Although you believe yourself weak, changing a pattern which has existed for generations requires immense strength and insight, and you are to be admired and recognized for this.

You did not deserve what was done to you, and you do not deserve to live with the effects of those experiences. Indeed, you deserve love and abundance, as do all beings. Beliefs and fears you carry as a result of your experiences are presenting obstacles to attaining the fullness of the love and abundance available to you, and it is our hope that you will begin to counter these obstacles and move forward despite them or even without them.

We encourage you to look within as you begin or progress in this journey, for as you heal, you will discover that the wounds run deeper than you realize. This does not mean it is a hopeless endeavor, however. It merely means that you will need to be cognizant of what arises as you progress. You will clear one block or heal one smaller wound only to discover more beneath, and it will be necessary for you to be prepared to address what you uncover.

Necessity aside, however, it is always your choice whether to address any issue you recognize. It is, as we have stated, entirely your choice whether to even begin this journey, and how or whether to proceed with it. There are no set-in-stone requirements. There is no "right" or "wrong" way to begin or proceed. All is subject to your choice.

Remember that you need not make these choices alone, with no support. Nor do you make them in isolation, for the choices you make will affect those around you and by extension many others. It is a ripple effect that can bring further healing to your world if this is the path you choose.

Healing the world, however, is not the wisest priority for you. It is wisest that your first priority be yourself. Your own healing and awareness. Your growth. As much as you may wish to heal the world, and as much power as you may have to do so, healing must begin with you. Attempting to repair another's wound while losing your own blood does not serve anyone. Tend first to your wounds, but know that as you do so, you will facilitate healing for others.

In time, you will recognize the progress you make and have

already made. In time, you may begin to consciously work with others to facilitate their healing while continuing on your own journey. The amount of time this path will take cannot be stated, for it will differ for each of you and there are many variables. Ultimately, however, the amount of time your journey will take is subject to the choices you make.

Your power to choose, to learn, and to heal is immense even if you are currently unaware of it. It lives within you waiting for you to reconnect with it, for it has never been stolen from you or lost, merely obscured. It is safe now for you to uncover that power and learn to use it to benefit yourself and others. Although this prospect may be frightening to you, it is one which will bring abundance into your life if you choose.

In all things, we hope that you will remember you are not alone. Other humans have had harmful experiences; it is not something exclusive to you because of some flaw within you. There are no flaws. Perhaps there are behaviors and patterns you would be wise to change, but there are no flaws, and certainly none that would render you deserving of harm.

You may have people around you who are willing and able to support you in this journey. It is our hope that this is so, whether those people are family, friends, or professionals. If you have no one, we encourage you to reach out to a professional who may be able to assist you. However, we also encourage you to look to your friends and loved ones and determine objectively whether any of them might be a support if you are willing to ask. At times, you may believe you have no support, but the truth is that those around you are unaware of your need or are aware but waiting to be asked before attempting to aid you.

And your guides are with you. Indeed, not only your own guides, for through your reading of this book we have now encountered you and are aware of you. If you are not yet consciously connected with your guides and do not know their names, you may call upon one of us in a time you feel alone. To the best of our ability, we shall respond, though depending upon your awareness you may not recognize our responses.

This book may serve as a resource for you as you progress in your journey, for you will gain different understanding of our words at later stages. Each time you make progress, you will learn more about the journey and yourself, and you will begin to restore the connections with your core Self and inner power. Viewing this book through a different lens over time may lead to different understanding that may in turn lead to further healing.

However you choose to take this journey, and indeed whether you choose it at all, you are asked to remember that you are a vital piece of the Universal Whole. Even at times when you feel unworthy or as if you do not matter, your presence is valued and your absence would be noticed. You are needed, you are wanted, and you are loved.

River's Closing Message

J first conceived of this book because of the daily channeled messages I post on Facebook, some of which seemed very relevant to trauma survivors. As I noted in my introduction, Shiva and Pietkela had ideas other than simply compiling those messages and adding some new material. The topics of the messages were incorporated into the book, and at a few points I included a paragraph or two from one of the messages if Shiva and Pietkela indicated that doing so was appropriate.

At one time, I had thought about writing a book of my own to encourage and support trauma survivors, and I may still do that in the future. This book, though, is entirely channeled aside from my introduction and this closing message. It's one thing to hear a human say you can heal and you didn't deserve what happened to you. Hearing it from higher-level beings is something else entirely. For me, at least, sometimes hearing it from the higher-level beings gets through in a way hearing it from humans can't.

I've been on my own healing journey for quite some time now, because healing isn't something that's going to happen overnight. Sometimes I've stalled out because I didn't have the support I needed from other humans or because I was trying to heal wounds from the past while living in a traumatizing present. Fortunately, I'm in a place now where my daily life isn't traumatizing, and I've been able to direct more time and energy to my healing overall.

I've had times when I've felt as if I was regressing. Times when my behavior was unquestionably harmful or at least hurtful to those closest to me. I don't make excuses for those times; even though I was struggling with my own pain and trauma, and at times legitimately didn't know how else to behave, there are never excuses for causing harm to anyone else. Only reasons. The reasons don't make it okay.

Some of the people I affected chose to remove themselves from my life, and I completely support their decision. With those who remain, I have discussed this and have made apologies and amends as possible. I'm still in that process, and I'm finding that the more I accept responsibility for my behavior without allowing myself to fall into the tar pit of guilt and self-hatred, the more I heal.

I've also had times when healing seemed impossible or when depression and other mental health issues led me to just plain not feel like trying anymore. I used to get angry with myself at those times. I said some pretty horrible things to myself in judgment and condemnation.

Over time, and with support, I've learned to be compassionate with myself when I hit those lows. The way my brain works is not a choice, and the effects some of the dysfunctions have on me are also not things I choose. These times still happen, but I've reached a point in my journey where I'm able to say, "This sucks, and I don't like it, but I know it will pass and I know it isn't my fault I feel this way."

In contrast, I've also had times during which I've made immense progress. Times when I've been able to recognize the effects of trauma in my behavior and thought patterns and change those patterns. I've been able to reconnect, at least to an extent, with my inner power and my core Self, and I learn more every day about who I am beneath the trauma and the "sludge" of my past. For me, that's huge; I went through a lot of my life with no clue who I was.

The healing journey is a process. A long one, and sometimes a painful or frightening one. It's easy to want to stay in your current state; that seems simpler, even if you recognize that it isn't benefiting you or anyone else. It seems less scary. And as Shiva and Pietkela pointed out, that is a choice you can make.

But if you choose to begin or continue your healing journey, even when it seems difficult or impossible, you will change. You will grow. Most importantly, those wounds will heal.

I share pieces of my story in this book in the hope of showing that healing is possible, and to show that you really aren't alone, no matter how isolated you might feel.

If you're on your healing journey, or are ready to begin it, please reach out for support. As you progress, you may encounter memories that you'll need help to process and handle. You also might benefit from having someone cheering you on and reflecting to you that you really are changing and improving at the times when you feel like you aren't getting anywhere. Energy healing, channeling, coaching…all of those have their place, but unless the practitioner you're working with is also a licensed mental health professional, they can only do so much. I strongly recommend that anyone who is on a journey of healing from trauma seek the support of a licensed professional as well as, or instead of, other healing modalities and practices.

However, what works best for you is what's right for you. When considering any type of support, you know best what you need, and you know if something works or not.

On the next couple of pages, I share some resources I've found that might be of benefit to you. This is not a recommendation of any of them; I simply offer them for you to consider. Following the resource list, I share the channeled daily messages that sparked this project.

You deserve to be well. You deserve to be loved. I hope this book has helped you in your journey in some way.

Resources

This is far from an exhaustive list. If none of these feel relevant or workable for you, please know that others exist, and research will help you find them.

Hotlines:

NOTE: Many of the hotlines listed here are exclusive to the United States. Similar hotlines may exist in other countries.

National (USA) Suicide Prevention Lifeline: 988 https://suicidepreventionlifeline.org/

Talk Suicide Canada: call 211 or 1-833-456-4566; or text 45645 from 4pm-12am Eastern time

Crisis Textline: Text "HOME" to 741741 https://www.crisistextline.org/

National (USA) Domestic Violence Hotline: 1-800-799-7233 https://www.thehotline.org/

The Trevor Project (for LGBTQ+ people under age 25): 1-866-488-7386 https://www.thetrevorproject.org/

Trans Lifeline (for transgender and nonbinary people):1-877-565-8860 https://translifeline.org/
(In Canada: 1-877-330-6366)

National (USA) Sexual Assault Hotline: 1-800-656-4673 https://www.rainn.org/about-national-sexual-assault-telephone-hotline

Websites:

Trauma Survivors Network https://www.traumasurvivorsnetwork.org/pages/home

Anxiety & Depression Association of America https://adaa.org/

Trauma Center at JRI (NOTE: This page has links to other resources) https://jri.org/services/behavioral-health-and-trauma/trauma-center

Books:

The Courage to Heal by Ellen Bass & Laura Davis, 4th edition, HarperCollins, ©2008

The Complex PTSD Workbook by Arielle Schwartz, PhD, Althea Press, ©2016

Trauma-Sensitive Mindfulness by David Treleaven, W.W. Norton & Company, ©2018

The Body Keeps the Score by Bessel van Der Kolk, M.D., Penguin Books, ©2014

The Original Channeled Messages

NOTE: These messages are presented in the order in which they originally appeared as daily messages on Facebook. I have not edited or revised them. Some are channeled from Shiva and some from Pietkela; I have not indicated which are which.

Love surrounds you. Yet some of you reject it. You find yourselves unworthy of love. You judge yourselves harshly, and sadly, this judgment extends to others.

Before you can truly embrace life and the others who live alongside you, you must clear away the self-hatred. Learning to see clearly who you are and what dwells within you is no easy task. For some, it will take years. For some, it is a journey upon which you will be for the remainder of your life.

However, I urge you to take the first steps of this journey. To seek healing within yourself. Some who call themselves healers are, in truth, deeply wounded inside, and are not tending to their own wounds before attempting to tend to others.

Be one who tends to your own wounds first. Seek the help you need to heal the damage within. No one is irreparably damaged. Within each of you dwells the perfect being as which you were created. One need not be "fully healed" to work to heal others; this is, in fact, nearly impossible. But one must be tending to one's own wounds before endeavoring to tend to others.

You have the power to heal. Exercise this power first upon yourself.

***

How can you look upon yourself and see not beauty, but ugliness? How can you cast this ugliness upon others?

Yet this is what some humans choose to do. To see within themselves that which they hate and fear, and cast these things upon others as an excuse to hate and fear them as well. Some cannot embrace their true selves, and to cover up that which is too painful to face, they accuse others of possessing these qualities they themselves possess.

No one is deserving of hatred. Regardless of one's appearance, beliefs, or past, no one deserves to be held in a view which negates their very existence. For all those who carry even a spark of love and humanity, hatred destroys with no hope of new creation.

And yet some of you turn this hatred, this destruction, upon yourselves, and believe yourselves unworthy of love or redemptions. Beloveds, if you were truly beyond these things, you would not hold this belief, for love and redemption would be the furthest things from your minds. The fact that you fear yourself unworthy is a sign that you are, indeed, worthy and able to receive.

Your healing begins when you cease to view yourself as damaged beyond healing. Believe you can heal, and so it shall be.

***

How wonderful you are.

When you read those words, do you dispute them? In your mind, is a voice speaking contradictions and denials?

Beloveds, why do you doubt yourselves so? The Source from which you come created you to be beautifully, wonderfully made, and yet you believe yourself to be ugly and worthless.

Raise your heads. Look toward the sky. The sun and moon. Look around you at nature. Visit the sea or lake or river. Are these not wonderfully made?

They come from the same Source as you. If they are beautiful and wonderful, how can you be otherwise?

See yourself as you are, not as others and events in your life have led you to believe.

***

There are those among you who question whether you have the "right," for want of better terms, to remove people from your life when they have wronged you or caused you harm.

I assure you, your life is your own. When another has become toxic to you, or persists in knowingly causing you pain or damage, they have no right to remain within your sphere.

Your life is your own, and who is or is not part of that life is solely your choice.

I hear you now. "But they are family. But he is my husband. But she is my partner." Do you truly wish to allow these roles to be held by someone who would intentionally cause you pain?

Your health, both physical and mental, matters more than ties of blood or legality. You may, of course, choose to allow these people to remain, but there is no requirement to do so. Do you not deserve a life free of toxins and hate?

Make the wisest choice in your highest ideal. And, for those who need these words, remember that family is not blood, not legalities; it is those who love and accept one another without condition. And it can be chosen.

***

Nothing which has occurred in your life has truly changed you. You have changed, yes, but those changes were not created by others or by events. Those changes come from within you.

When harm occurs, it does alter how you see the world. It alters how you see yourself. And these things cause it to appear that you yourself have been altered.

Within you is the core, the shining light around which your physical form was created. This core, this light, has not been dulled or damaged. This light still shines within you, and although you might not see it, it shines brightly for those who truly see.

Know that this light is there, and know that you carry it regardless of harm your past has caused you.

Seek this light within you, for that is the first step toward seeing it within others.

Know this light is there, and embrace it, for some of you fear it instead.

Know your true self, and healing shall occur.

***

Among you today are those who need this message more than others: You are loved. You are needed. You are valued. You, above all others, are unique in the Universe, and your presence brings light and joy. Your absence, though you believe otherwise, would be noted with sadness and pain.

You have fallen into a darkness of late, and this darkness convinces you that light does not exist anywhere, let alone within you. But I assure you that light is there.

Reach up out of the darkness. Seek the hands of those who will help you find the light once again.

You are loved. You are needed. You are wanted.

You are alive. We need you to remain so.

You are not alone.

***

How can you look upon yourself and not see the light and beauty within? For those who are outside of you, those things are so bright, so clear, that it seems impossible not to see.

Yet some of you struggle to see these things within yourself.

Some of you have, in fact, been taught that those things do not exist within you, and therefore do not even think to look.

They are there. You carry light. You carry beauty. And you are wonderfully created.

Learn to look for and look at the light within you. What others have told you is false. You are beautiful.

***

Remember who you are. At times, you forget this. You forget that you were created as a wonderful expression of Source. That you were created with power, strength, and grace. You forget that you carry light and beauty within you.

Remember who you are. Remember the power within you. Remember that you are worthy of love and abundance, and that when you recognize this, no one shall take these things from you.

Remember who you are. Honor yourself. Respect the person you are, have been, and will become. Know that you are where you need to be at this time, and that you are not the things you have done or experienced.

Remember who you are.

***

You are so deserving of love, and yet you reject love when it is offered to you. You reject it within yourself. Why is this so?

For those of you who have experienced harm at the hands--or words--of others, the answer is clear. You reject love because you have been taught or shown that you are unworthy of it. But that is false. Nothing about you has rendered you unworthy. That belief is only the remnants of others' harm.

Open your eyes and heart to the love around and within you. The love that you feel for others belongs to you as well. Allow yourself to receive it, both from others and from yourself.

You are abundantly worthy. Nothing any has said or done can

change this.

***

For some of you, the concept of having power in your life, and having the power to change the world, is frightening. It need not be so. You are not obligated to use your power for anything. You may choose simply to say you are powerless, and this choice is valid, though the statement is untrue. However, if you believe it to be true, so it is, while remaining equally false.

For some of you, power itself is frightening. You have seen others misuse and abuse their power in ways that have harmed you and others. Know that power used to harm is not true power.

True power lies within each of you. Each of us, for it exists in all beings, not only humans. This is the power to change. To create. To bring darkness out of the shadows and shed light upon it, for though darkness and light do and must coexist, bringing darkness into the light allows change to occur.

Release the fear of your own power. Learn to embrace that power. Learn to create your life and world as you wish to live.

***

Why do you refuse to trust yourself? Actions others have committed against you are no flaw or fault of yours. Unwise choices you have made in your life and likewise not fault or flaw. They are simply things which have occurred.

"But I have harmed others," you say, and that may be so. However, if you are aware of what you have caused and feel remorse for doing so, why do you not trust yourself to avoid those actions in the future?

Trust is the foundation upon which love and power are built. While love and power and entwined, without trust, the rest falls into the sea, as it were.

Examine the areas in which you distrust yourself. Why has this distrust developed? How can you change it?

Know that your guides are with you on this journey and will assist you if asked. Call upon them and upon others for whom you do feel trust to help you regain and build the trust in yourself.

***

Do you know how valuable you are? I speak not in terms of your value to others, but simply the value that is yours and is you by virtue of your existence.

Each action you take, each thought, each word, affects more than only you. Words you speak or write may reach people you will never know. The energy you put out may bring about profound change in other areas of the Universe. A single tiny action might ripple into massive change and growth.

Refrain from diminishing yourself. Resist the belief that you are insignificant or small. Each being, each consciousness, has a role to play in the Whole of the Universe.

You are one, but you are infinite. Know this to be true, and treat yourself as the incredible, valuable being you are. Allow love, both from within and from outside yourself.

***

Your feelings are valid.

For some of you, that is a phrase you may not have heard before, or have not heard enough in your life. You have been told you are "wrong" to feel as you feel, or that your feelings have no basis and are therefore invalid.

I tell you that if you feel, however you feel, it is true for you and therefore is valid.

Choose carefully how you respond or react to the feelings that arise within you, for it is in actions and words that pain and harm may lie, or that choices may be made that are unwise or damaging. Actions and words can be unwise.

But emotions are part of being human, and they are valid. You are valid. Allow yourself to feel as you feel, and reject statements by others that your feelings are not allowed or are not "right."

***

For whom do you feel love? Many among you would name family, whether blood or chosen. Some would name friends or partners.

How many of you would name yourselves?

In the process of learning and engaging with the world around you as a small child, some of you have learned to love others at the cost of yourselves. Others of you have learned to love yourselves at the cost of others. Learn now to love yourself *and* others, and know there is no cost.

Love is an infinite. There are no limits. There is no "running out." Love exists everywhere, in and for all beings.

There is no need to exclude yourself from receiving it. There is no need to exclude others from it. You as an individual need not love all others, of course. Particularly when one has harmed you, you need not feel love for them, or indeed feel anything at all. But throughout the Universe, love is available for all.

Hatred is not the opposite of love. Hatred is negation and destruction. To hate is to deny the right to exist. Why would you choose to feel this for any being? How does it serve you?

How does it serve you to feel hatred for yourself? Do you not deserve to exist?

Examine within yourself the existence of love and hatred. Choose which you would prefer, and which would best serve you. And above all, learn, if you have not already, to feel love for yourself, for you to deserve to exist.

***

In your world, there are those who seek to harm or damage others. It is a sad fact of human life that this is so.

However, when you have been harmed, often you see harm where none exists. You project upon others the fears and damage which have been caused to you, and assume malevolent intentions where there are no such intentions.

Awaken from that fear. Part of your work in healing from harm and trauma is to learn to recognize when ill intent truly exists, and when it is your own mind and fear playing tricks upon you.

When there truly is harm or malevolent intent, take steps to protect yourself. But first discern objectively whether this malevolence is real, or is the effect of what has gone before in your life.

Work to assume positive intent until shown otherwise from those who have not been involved in causing you harm. Work to assume positive intent on your own part in the actions and words you choose.

This is part of healing. And you are not alone in this work.

***

For some of you, now is a time for facing your own darkness. Your "shadow self," as some term it.

As you progress in this work, be mindful of identifying yourself as your shadow, rather than identifying the shadow as part of your Self.

You are not the darkness. You are, rather, a perfect, harmonious balance of darkness and light, as is all Creation. This is something you have forgotten or of which you have lost sight, but it is true. The work of this time is to reclaim that harmony, that balance; it is not to eliminate the darkness or shadow, but to incorporate it and claim it as part of you.

But at the same time, light is part of you as well. You are not the shadow, not the light; you are both, in a complete, glorious whole that mirrors the Whole of Creation.

This is the work you are called to. Recognizing, incorporating, and honoring all aspects of yourself, while knowing that you are not the aspects but rather are the whole.

***

Each of you has a place in the Universe. In the world. Most importantly, in your own life.

Sometimes as humans you lose sight of your place. You believe you have no place, no right to exist. You believe that you do not fit or belong.

I tell you that this is an illusion. Each of you is part of the glorious Whole that comprises the Universe. Were you to not exist, the Universe would not be as it is. You are integral, even should you be unaware of this.

Recognize your place. Recognize that you are needed.

***

Healing is not a linear path, and yet some of you treat it as such. You condemn or reject those who are not constantly making forward progress in their journeys--even when that person is you yourself.

All journeys have twists and turns. Healing particularly, for as you heal one part of yourself, other parts which need healing will become evident. Other issues which hold you back or cause you pain will come to the fore.

Accept that healing is a journey which will occupy the remainder of your life, and accept and honor that at times, this journey may appear to have stopped or even reversed. Accept this, and show compassion to those--including yourself--who have chosen to undertake a healing journey, for this is not a journey for the faint of heart. Healing takes courage. Refrain from underestimating this.

***

Among you there are those who become angry or fearful when things do not go as planned. This is an effect of your pasts, but also of your expectations. You are not expected to complete everything. You need not take on the responsibilities for everything in the world.

Yet you believe yourselves responsible for so much that is outside of your responsibility, and you condemn yourselves when your plans do not reach fruition or when you are unable to rise to the impossible tasks you have set before yourselves.

Beloveds, show yourselves compassion. Your measure is not the number of things you accomplish or the accolades and certifications you achieve. You are abundantly worthy of love solely by virtue of your existence.

Let your measure be the good you place into the world rather than numbers and pieces of paper. For you yourselves are your own measure.

***

Gratitude is a concept sometimes misused or misunderstood by humans.

When one expresses gratitude, it is felt and appreciated. But one need not express gratitude for what has caused harm or pain.

At times, it is said that one should "thank" the negative experiences in their life, and even "thank" their abusers, for providing life lessons. And for some of you, that is impossible. You cannot feel gratitude for being harmed or damaged.

This is acceptable. You need not feel or express gratitude for that which has harmed you. You need not seek to find "lessons" in damage that has been done to you.

Gratitude is something you may choose, or not. It is something which is entirely individual to each of you. None may tell you that you "must" feel gratitude. It is a choice you have available to make.

Choose what feels most helpful and healing to you, and release the "musts" and "shoulds."

***

The first true step in the journey of your life is to know yourself.

This is a step at times overlooked or negated. You may be taught that you must choose your career path, your schooling, even your hobbies and social activities, based upon what others think. You are not taught to know who you are at your core, but who others want you to be.

In a healing journey, particularly, one needs to begin with knowing that core self. You cannot heal to become who you truly are if you are unaware of who you are at your core. That *is* who you truly are; how can you become this if you do not know what it is?

Spend time in connection with yourself. This may be through meditation, or simply sitting quietly. It may be through journaling, or reading books that call to you. It may be through communication with your guides or even through divination tools.

Whatever method works for you, I encourage and invite you to use it to gain a clearer understanding of your core self. This will benefit you greatly in your journey and in your work in the world.

***

Give yourself compassion at this time. No matter what you are struggling with, no that it is temporary; however, know also that it is acceptable to feel sadness or fear about the struggles.

You have learned to deny yourself the right to feel. It is time now to turn within and connect with your emotions. Creating abundance, creating positivity, necessitates a combination of reason and emotion. Denying or negating either one will lead to difficulties in building the life you wish to live.

Connect with yourself and know that emotions, whether positive or negative, are not the enemy. They are part of existence, and you are allowed to feel them.

***

Of late, there has seemed a tendency for humans to judge one another's experiences and dismiss those experiences which do not match their own.

This is harmful and even damaging to others. No two people--no two beings of any type--experience or perceive everything in exactly the same manner. One person may experience severe trauma from something which merely causes another a minor inconvenience. One person may communicate with beings they identify as angels, while another communicates with beings of light. One may heal from their trauma through discussing it and connecting with others who have experienced trauma, while another copes with their trauma by refusing to speak of it.

Your ways are valid as long as they cause no harm to yourself or others. But others' ways are equally valid as long as they cause no harm.

Refrain from judging and negating others' experiences because they are not your own. Accept and honor that all beings have unique perspectives and perceptions, and that all of these are true for the individuals who have them.

***

Refrain from making yourself responsible for all people and things within your life. You are not alone in all things. When you act as if you are the only one able or competent to complete certain tasks or accomplish certain things, you do a disservice to the others who are there to aid you, and to yourself as you place more pressure upon yourself than is needed.

Examine the tasks in your life. Identify those which may be passed on to others, or which may be unnecessary at all.

You are one person, and although you are limitless within, limits such as time and physical capacity do exist. Be mindful of these.

Above all, remember that you are more important than the tasks on any list. You matter more than the things you do.

***

Some of you have been taught that seeking help is shameful. That you must do for yourselves, and that you are solely responsible whether you succeed or fail. You have been taught that illness is weakness, and that need is undesirable.

None of these things are truth. They are fictions passed along from generation to generation by those who were too fearful or stubborn to understand that no one need struggle alone.

Reaching out for help is no cause for shame. It is strength, for asking for help requires the strength to trust. Illness is not weakness, it is merely a limitation of your physical form. Failure is an illusion; there is no failure, there is only growth and learning, although you may grow and learn things you did not foresee or desire.

Learn to release the fear and shame of seeking help when it is needed. Learn to show the strength to say, "I need help."

This is a way of connecting, and as you are helped, so shall you help others in time.

***

Those who seek to silence you about your experiences and emotions are those who struggle with their own.

None has the right to prevent you from speaking your truth, whatever that truth may be. When another strives to silence you, or coerces you into speaking only in a certain way or thinking only certain thoughts, this is incorrect action on their part and is an attempt by them to control that which they struggle to control within themselves.

Negative emotions do not prevent the creation of positive events and occurrences. Light and darkness, positivity and negativity, these things must coexist for the Universe to remain in balance--and for each individual to maintain balance in their own lives and creations.

Allow yourselves to speak. Do so in gentle, nonharmful ways, but allow it nonetheless, for through speaking truth comes healing.

***

Look within yourself for the love you seek. Love surrounds you, though you may be unaware of it, but you cannot accept this until you are willing to accept the love within yourselves.

You love others freely, for it is possible to love others without feeling love for yourself. However, until you love yourself fully and freely, you will struggle to accept love from others. You will struggle to accept the love of the Creator.

You feel unloved though you are surrounded by love, and you do not realize that you feel unloved because you have not yet learned to love yourself.

It is time to begin this lesson.

***

How have you rejected the Self within you?

When one experiences harmful or painful incidents, at times the very aspect of the self that had this experience is buried and rejected. This is a mechanism for protection, but it causes further harm. If you reject part of yourself, how can others accept you fully?

This is not something you do intentionally, but it causes no less harm for its unintentional nature.

Learn to embrace yourself. The parts of you that have experienced harm and pain are there, waiting to be loved and embraced. This is not easy work, but for true healing to occur, it is necessary.

Know that you need not take on this work alone. Supports exist for you. Seek them, and accept aid when offered.

You are worthy of love. Will you give this gift to yourself?

***

When trauma occurs, a part of your Self becomes frozen in that moment. These frozen thought-forms, these child-like consciousnesses, then become the parts of you which you reject or attempt to deny.

Your experiences do not create who you are, but they do form the basis for how you are in the world. By embracing and loving these "children" within you, healing begins and progresses.

No part of you is beyond healing. No part of you is hopeless or unworthy. But to receive all that of which you are abundantly deserving, you first need provide it for yourself. You need to provide these inner children with the love and acceptance they have been denied for so long.

Seek aid in this work, for pain may occur, and memories may arise with which you will need support. Find the help you need. But I encourage you to take up this work, for the benefits will be immeasurable.

***

Many of you who have experienced harm and trauma have had times of believing you are alone. That no other has had experiences such as yours. That only you are "broken" or "damaged."

Know that this is not so. You are not alone.

Know, too, that as you progress toward healing, you are not alone in this work. Your guides are with you always. These beings, though unseen and perhaps unknown to you, have not left you and are waiting to aid you when you are ready.

Other humans exist who can work with you to assist your progress in your healing journey.

You have never been alone, though it has often felt otherwise. Trust now in the presence of love and the presence of those who wish to support you. Trust that you can become who you wish to be.

***

Healing is a journey. At times, it is a long one, one on which you feel isolated and without support.

Know that as you make this journey, you are not alone. Others who are on their journeys likewise feel alone, but collectively, you are many.

Those who are on their own healing journeys do not lose anything by your need for support. There is no time when love and assistance run dry, as it were.

Some of you hold back from seeking assistance on your journeys because you believe somehow that you are taking away support from others. Know that this is not so.

Seek the help and support you need. There is no shame in needing to heal. There is no wrongness in needing support.

You are worthy of being whole, beloveds, for in truth you have always been whole. Parts of you have been harmed, but that does not change you at your core.

Seek the aid you require to reconnect with your core Self and make the journey, for this will benefit you greatly.

***

You are under no obligation to maintain connections with any other human.

Often, it is said that you must keep ties with another because they are related to you, or because you work with them, or for any number of other reasons. This is not the case. If a connection with another causes you pain, or if it is a situation that brings toxicity or harm into your life, you need not maintain that connection.

Some connections are easier to sever than others, but you do not owe anyone a place in your life, regardless of who they are.

Form connections that bring you peace. Connections with those with whom there is mutual respect and support. And remove the connections that bring you difficulty and pain.

This is not a command but a choice you may make, for your life is your own, and the choice of who is part of that life is also your own.

***

Tend to your healing. Tend to your health and well-being.

Some in your life may state that you must devote your time and energy to those around you at the cost of yourself. This is false. While it is not advisable to take away from others, it is even less advisable to take away from yourself. Do you not deserve to heal?

You are not removing anything from others if you choose to devote your time and energy to improving your life. You are the ultimate creative power in your life, and it is acceptable to use this power to create benefit for yourself.

If you choose to give your energy to others at the cost of yourself, you cannot truly bring benefit to them, for you must care for yourself in order to be able to care for others. If you are constantly drained and depleted, how can you provide for anyone?

Tend to your healing, and know that you are abundantly deserving of creating a positive life for yourself. You have this power.

***

You have been told that you must set aside your anger. That you are not permitted to feel certain emotions about your experiences or the people who were involved.

I encourage you, rather than forbidding emotions, to allow yourself to experience them.

The ability to feel emotions is one of the most profound powers given to humans. It is what makes you human. Emotions are part and parcel of who you are.

Feeling an emotion does not mean reacting in a negative way or choosing harmful actions or words. It means allowing the experience to occur and gifting yourself with the compassion to permit yourself to be human.

Emotions are not the enemy. You are not evil or "wrong" for feeling negatively toward experiences and people that have harmed you. But if you forbid yourself to feel and deny yourself that part of human experience, you are furthering the harm.

Allow emotions. Do so in nonharmful ways, but allow the emotions to exist, and embrace yourself as you feel them.

***

When we speak of the power each being has to create their own life, we do not mean that you choose to create experiences which have harmed you. We do not mean that you somehow created or chose the actions of others that caused you pain.

You carry within you the power to create, yet often are unaware that this power exists, and so do not utilize it. The power you have to create your life informs your own actions and choices when you are aware of how to exercise that power. It does not bring evil or harm into your life; it provides means to bring benefit and love when you are aware of how this power may be used.

Some have twisted the meaning of the statement "you create your reality" into victim-blaming and cruel rhetoric that furthers abuse and harm. This is not the intention of the phrase--or of the creative power you carry within you.

In your healing journey, you may learn to embrace your creative power and use it to bring healing and benefit to your life. This is a choice you may make. But even should you choose not to embrace this power, still you do not create others' negative choices toward you.

You did not create the harm that was done to you. Any who says otherwise is speaking falsely.

***

The work of healing, the work of creating your most beneficial life, the work of becoming who you wish to be...all of these are valid and valuable courses to take.

Yet do not dismiss the importance of the work of rest.

This seems a contradiction, yet for some of you, allowing yourself to rest requires more effort than the other work combined.

Balance is needed in all things. The work of living a human life is no different. Between resting and working, balance is vital.

***

You know yourself, and yet you doubt this knowledge. When another tells you who you are, tells you their perception of you, at times you internalize what they say.

This is unnecessary and is harmful to your sense of self. No one can tell you who you are. No one knows you better than you know yourself. Although you may have lost touch with this inner knowing, it still is there. You still know who you are.

Spend time engaging in self-study. As a child, you knew your true self, yet as you grew, others convinced you that you were wrong. Spend time now relearning what you knew as a child.

Nothing that has occurred in your life has taken away your ability to know your true self. Nothing has erased that self from existence. Experiences and the words of others may have obscured your true self, but they have not erased it.

Take this time. Reconnect with your core. Find the love within you once again.

***

Many times, people are blamed for things which have been done to them. People are told they have chosen to be harmed, that they have a "lesson to learn," or that it is something they have manifested through "low vibration."

None of these things are true.

When one person harms another, it is not the fault or

responsibility of the one who was harmed. Each human has free will. Each person chooses their actions. If one chooses to cause harm, that is their choice and therefore their responsibility.

Stating that someone who has been harmed is at fault is, itself, abusive behavior. You are furthering the harm and pain the person has already experienced by informing them they have chosen it.

You are, of course, free to believe what you wish to believe, for free will includes that freedom. However, I encourage you to refrain from telling someone who has trusted you enough to come forward with a story of abuse and harm that they chose it or wanted it, for that does not benefit them and shows you to be as harmful as people in that person's past.

***

Your healing journey is your own. No other may tell you how to accomplish it.

I have stated this in the past, yet many still believe they have the right to tell others how to heal from pain and harm. Many times, this is because they have been on their own healing journey and believe their way is the right way.

Your way of healing is right for you. However, it may not be right for all.

As you progress on your healing journey, know that others may come to you and state that you are doing it "wrong." That you must engage in certain activities, or believe certain things, or claim blame for what occurred. They may tell you that you are taking too long or that you are not taking long enough.

You may release their words, for they are not you, and your way of healing is valid provided it brings you benefit and harms no one. No one may tell you how you must heal, for your journey is yours and may proceed in the way that works for you.

You are not alone in this journey. Your guides are with you, ready to support you if asked. Other humans are available to support you, if you are able to reach out to them and trust them.

You are not alone, but the journey you undertake is solely yours to form and follow.

***

As your world gains greater understanding of the effects of experiences upon one's psyche, and indeed upon one's very sense of self, the process of healing will become easier.

As the world gains greater understanding of the reality that people who have experienced pain and trauma did not choose those experiences and do not consciously choose how they respond; as the world more fully understands that these responses and effects may linger for a lifetime even if the traumatic experiences have ended; healing will become more effective and will be embraced rather than rejected or ignored by those with no understanding.

I speak to those who have experienced any form of harm and live with the effects of it: You did not cause this. You did not choose it. And you are not beyond help or hope, though at times you feel as if you are.

Your healing journey is yours to choose, both the processes and, in fact, whether or not to undertake the journey at all. You do not follow this journey alone, however. Support from your guides, from other beings, and from other humans is here when you are ready to ask and receive it.

We who work with humans sorrow at what is done to some of you. You are loved, and you deserve to feel and experience love rather than pain.

You are not alone.

***

Do you believe you do not deserve to heal? That you do not have the right to be well?

Or is it that you believe you cannot heal, or will not know who you are if you are well?

When one embarks upon a healing journey, particularly when

one's sense of self has been warped or obscured by harmful experiences, it is a frightening choice and path. You are leaving familiarity, even if it is a familiarity with things you dislike or that continue to harm you, to step into the unknown.

Know that when you choose to step upon the path of this healing journey, you do so with the full love and support of your guides. Many of you also have love and support from humans around you, though you may be unaware of or resistant to this. Whether you choose to receive the love and support, however, it is there for you when you are ready to request and accept it.

Know, too, that as you progress upon your healing journey, at times it will not be easy. At times, it may seem to bring you more pain. But ultimately, it will bring you great benefit as you go and as you grow.

You have within you the power to heal. You have a true core Self that is who you are and who you will uncover as you progress. And you have the love and support of many, both seen and unseen.

***

The past is not something of which to "let go," but rather something to acknowledge.

This does not mean dwelling and wallowing in it, for that does not allow progress. Rather, it means that for some of you, "letting go" has become synonymous with denial and rejection, and this, too, does not allow progress.

Your past does not define you, but it has helped create you. You can change the effects it has had, but pretending your past does not exist serves no one, least of all you.

At times, too, even as you "let go" of your past, it refuses to let go of you. This may look like people from the past who will not leave you alone, or memories of the past that resurface at their own will. This is not a sign that you are not willing to let go or heal. It is the nature of trauma and of memory.

Acknowledge your past. Accept that it occurred and that it has affected you. You need not cling to it nor embrace it, but acknowledging and accepting are part of the path to healing.

***

You, and you alone, are in control of how you manage your past and your life. You, and you alone, have the choice of how and whether to address what has occurred in your past, of how to proceed with healing, of how to structure and create the life you wish to live.

This is immense power, yet it is power some of you deny or ignore. And of which some are unaware.

Others may guide you in your journey. They may offer suggestions. Those who are less beneficial to you may even direct you and issue commands. And yet none of these others may create your life or your healing for you.

Seek aid in your journey as you need, for reaching out for assistance is strength. Knowing when you are unable to proceed alone and require support is a sign of strength.

But know that ultimately, your journey is your own, and you have the power to progress upon it.

***

Some of you have been told that struggling with your past is a sign of weakness. Indeed, some have been told that this struggle is a sign that you do not wish to be well.

This is untrue. If you are wallowing and choosing to dwell upon your past, that is your choice, and may be a sign that you have not yet chosen to improve your life. However, if your past clings to you despite your best efforts; if you experience memories and effects against your will; this is not weakness. This is not a sign of your level of desire to heal.

Many things are within your control. However, after extreme events and traumas, some of that control is beyond your awareness, and you do not choose how your mind responds as a result.

Those who have survived damaging experiences inflicted upon them by others are not weak. Surviving these experiences requires immense strength. Choosing to proceed with your life, to try to create a positive life, to work toward healing--all of these are signs of strength.

You are strong. And you are loved.

***

You are abundantly loved. You are abundantly worthy of being treated with love and kindness.

Some of you will read those words and reject them, for it is not your experience. However, I assert that it is true. Even if you have not received the love of which you are so worthy, still you are worthy of it. Even if you deny the love of your guides, of the Creative Power, of other humans, still it is there for you when you are able to accept it.

Each of you is created with the capacity to give and receive abundantly. At the soul level, each of you does so. The shift to denial, to rejection, to hoarding your emotions and resources, comes upon incarnation, as does the choice some make to cause harm to others.

All beings are created with free will. The other qualities and capacities with which you are created are subject to that will. Although you may hold within you abundant love, you have a choice of whether to express that love, share it, or keep it to yourself. Likewise, although you are worthy of receiving abundant love, you may choose to reject it or deny it.

It is our hope that you will choose to open to the possibility of giving and receiving love. It is our hope that you will become aware of your core self, the Self that is abundantly deserving of all good things, and that you will accept that this Self is who you truly are.

***

Some of you speak of healing the world, or your country, or a situation in your environment.

While this desire is admirable, I encourage you to first turn your attention to healing yourself.

Some of you seek to heal others, whether on an individual or global scale, out of a true wish to help and express love. Others of you do so to ignore your own need for healing, or because you deny you have anything left to heal within yourself. Denial of pain and struggle is not healing.

Choosing to use your gifts to bring about healing on a broader scale is not wrong, but if you are not progressing upon your journey to heal from your own experiences, the healing you bring to others will be less effective and may not benefit you or them.

Some humans state, "You cannot heal others until you are healed." This is false, and gives rise to the many who obscure their struggles or deny they need to heal, for they so much wish to heal others that they pretend--or even delude themselves--that they have no inner healing left to do.

A truer statement would be, "You must make continued progress upon your healing journey in order to be effective in helping others heal." For all of you carry gifts which can bring about healing; however, it is most beneficial to use those gifts for your own growth and benefit first.

***

Be gentle with yourself as you progress on your healing journey. Healing is not as straightforward as you may wish it to be or as some claim. You will progress, yet at times you will feel as if you have fallen back to your starting point or even lower.

Each time you make progress, you go further than before. Each time you fall back, you fall back less far, though it may appear otherwise.

You have grown. You have made incredible changes. You--and other humans around you--may not always be aware of these changes, for some of them are subtle and within you and are not visible to the outer eye. But know that the changes and growth have occurred. You are not the person you were even days or weeks ago.

Each time you consciously choose to walk the healing path rather than remain stagnant, you are healing yourself. Each time you consciously choose to embrace your inner power and confront the things you wish or need to change, you are growing.

Be gentle with yourself--and be proud of yourself, for you are stronger and have made more progress than you know.

***

Allow yourself, for one moment, to envision the life you most wish for yourself. Where would you live? With whom would you surround yourself?

Who would you be?

This last question can be frightening for some, for you do not know who you are now, and the thought of who you might become if things change is more than you feel able to manage at this time.

Know that who you are now may be obscured, but you are the person you were created to be. This person may be hidden beneath layers of pain and harm, yet they still exist within you.

The person you would be if you lived the life you most wish is that core person. The person within you, beneath those layers.

You have the power within you to become that person once again. To work to heal from your past, though this is work that will never be completed, for healing is a journey rather than a finite ending. Yet healing is possible.

Know that you, at your core, have never changed from the person you wish to be, and you may find that person again with work, with help and support as needed. You are not alone.

***

Where you are now in your life is acceptable and valid.

Where you wish to be in your life is acceptable and valid.

You are not lessened by your experiences, nor by any difficulties which arise as a result of those experiences.

You are not "less than" others who have not had similar experiences, or than those who have progressed further in their healing journeys than you have in yours.

You are you, beloveds. Abundantly loved, though you may not see or accept this love. Abundantly deserving of healing, of creating a life in which you feel heard and accepted.

You may create this life. You may choose not to. You may reach out for support and assistance, or not. Whatever choices you make as you progress in your life, they are solely yours to make. Wherever you start, and however you grow, it is your choice.

Choose wisely, not based upon what others tell you, but upon who you deeply know yourself to be or wish to become. And know you are not alone.

***

For some of you, life has been a constant lesson in hiding and pretending. In obscuring who you are, not only from others but at times from yourself as well.

This is not a judgment, for you made those choices and learned that lesson to protect yourself against harm others may have inflicted upon you. This was not a conscious decision, but a protective mechanism created by your mind to keep you safe at times when safety did not exist.

If you are no longer in those times, those mechanisms no longer are required. Yet releasing them is not as simple as choosing. Just as you did not consciously create this protection, so it is difficult to consciously let it go. However, know that if you are in safety now, even if you do not fully perceive it, the time has come to release your mask. To cease pretending and begin the work of becoming your true self.

This work is not easy, yet it is abundantly rewarding, for each of you deserves to be who you truly are. This work may necessitate aid from others, and if you choose to begin the work and to request the aid, it shall be there for you.

You are wonderful. Do you not have a right to become the wonderful person you have always been?

***

You carry no blame for the experiences others have inflicted upon you. Any harm caused to you by others is their choice and responsibility, although they have claimed otherwise.

You do not choose the actions of others, only your own. You do not create or control what others choose to do; you have power only to create and control your own decisions and actions.

These words will not dissolve the guilt and blame you feel for what has occurred in your past, for that dissolution will take more time and more aid than simply words you read upon an electronic screen. Yet it is my hope that they shall enter your consciousness and begin the process of aiding you in releasing blame for something that has never been your fault.

There is no fault. There is no blame. There is only responsibility, and you are not responsible for what others have done.

***

At times, the choices you make in your life are affected by choices others have made. You act in ways which were exhibited to you in the past, ways which may have brought you pain or harm.

This is not a judgment, for certain actions and choices are imprinted upon you by choices made by others. You learn what you live, so to speak, and when you have lived in pain and fear, it is this which may drive your decisions.

I encourage you to release judgment of yourself for any pain or harm you have caused. Yet know that releasing judgment does not equate to releasing responsibility. If you have caused pain or harm to others through your actions, seek to acknowledge, to yourself and to those others where possible, your responsibility. To apologize and make amends if this is within your ability.

Know, too, that going forward you may take control of your actions. You may learn to recognize when you are embarking upon a course of action, when you are making choices, which are based upon what others have done to you in the past. You may learn to make alternate choices.

It is within your power to correct your course. I encourage you to embrace this power, for you need not continue to live imprisoned by what has occurred in your past.

***

As you progress in your healing journey, you will encounter obstacles. You will encounter resistance and fear. At times, you will stall or regress. And these occurrences may cause you to doubt your path, and, indeed, to doubt whether you are capable of healing.

This is work, beloveds, and yet it is work of which you are abundantly capable. A life journey, whether that of healing or of others facets of your life, is rarely, if ever, as straightforward as you would wish.

This journey shall be erratic at times. It is not a straight line, nor a single path, but rather a number of paths, each diverging at points of choice and decision.

At times, the path you choose may prove wrong for you; at those times, regression is necessary to return you to the correct path. Obstacles arise to give you time to consciously choose the next steps. Stalling allows you opportunity to examine where you are and where you have been, and perhaps to have respite for a short time from the journey.

You are not alone upon this journey, though you may be unaware of or resistant to the love and support available to you. Know, however, that love and support are here when you are willing to reach out for it.

Refrain from judging yourself for the route your healing journey takes, no matter how circuitous. It is your journey, and each step you take brings you closer to your true self.

***

Your healing journey is work. Each step you make necessitates conscious recognition of options, and conscious choice between those options.

At times, this journey becomes exhausting. And at those times, it is not only acceptable but advisable to rest.

No journey is accomplished without respite. When you travel, often you will stop, at least for a moment, to rest. So, too, does your healing journey require times of rest. While you may not entirely cease the work, you need not focus constantly upon it to the point of exhaustion. And if you reach that point, rest is needed, for you cannot progress if you are so tired you cannot see the progression before you.

Allow yourself these times of respite. Know that if you take rest, you shall not fall backward. Your journey shall not be undone by your choice to suspend progression upon it for a brief period. You will return to the journey when you have given yourself time to rest.

***

Heed what your bodies tell you. Some of you have become disconnected from your physical forms, whether through trauma or simply unawareness. Some of you are connected, but ignore the sensations and messages your body sends.

When you are not caring for your physical form, you are not caring for yourself. Although this form is transient in the grand scheme of things, still it is the form in which you will pass this lifetime, and it benefits you to tend to what it tells you.

Refrain from ignoring pain or illness. Although for some, obtaining medical care is difficult or nearly impossible, if you are able to seek it do so when needed. At the least, allow yourself to rest and recover when injury or illness strikes.

You live within this form, and you know, although may not be fully conscious of it, when something is not right. Heed this, and care for yourself as you are able, for you deserve to be cared for and well.

***

For some of you, the concept of "being in your body" is terrifying. Your body has experienced harm. It has experienced pain. You have no wish to be in it.

For others, your body is not the correct one in which to dwell. It is not matched with who you truly are.

Your body is the container in which your soul has chosen to pass this lifetime. It can be altered, but still it is yours.

Your feelings about your body are also yours, and are valid. Yet I encourage you, as you are able, to befriend this physical form in which you live. Connect at least with the parts of it that do not cause you pain or fear. Connect with the sensations it experiences. Connect with it as an aspect of your core Self, for in some ways it is the physical manifestation of that Self, even if some pieces of it have manifested incorrectly.

I will not tell you to "love your body"; for some of you, this is not yet possible, and I will not tell you to do something which will cause you additional stress. I merely invite you to befriend at least the parts of your body which do not bring you pain, and to remember that while your body is a manifestation of you, you are not defined by it. At your core, you are your Self, wonderfully created.

***

When one has experienced harm, it is a common reaction to reject what was harmed. To place blame upon the "past self" which had the experience, or to reject the part that was harmed.

Doing this, however, places an obstacle in the path to healing. It is difficult to heal from an experience you deny, or for which you take blame where none is warranted. It is difficult to progress toward well-being when you reject physical and mental aspects of yourself.

What has been done to you in the past is not your fault. There is no fault; there is no blame. There is only responsibility, and you are not responsible for the choices others have made to cause you harm.

You are not responsible for what others have done to you. They, and they alone, bear full responsibility for their choices.

If another spoke to you of their harmful experiences, would you reject them or deny their right to progress toward healing? If not, why do this to yourself?

I encourage you to work toward accepting those parts of yourself which you have rejected due to the harm they have experienced. To embrace the "past self" which is still suffering under the weight of those events.

You deserve to be well and loved, for you did not cause this harm.

***

Forgiveness, as often discussed, is not required to heal. You need not excuse the actions of others nor accept any apologies they may attempt to make. You need not even accept these others or their actions.

For healing, the path begins with forgiving yourself for the experiences. You are not, and never were, to blame for what others chose to do, and yet you cling to this blame, to identifying yourself as being at fault. This may not be conscious on your part, and yet at times your actions and your thoughts about yourself are guided by this mindset.

An important step--or steps, for this is a process which will continue throughout your healing journey--is to accept *yourself*, both as the person to whom these things happened and as the Self within you. To accept that you are not at fault, that you did not choose these actions.

And, most importantly, to accept that what others have chosen to do to you has not created you. It does not define you. You may choose to free yourself from those bonds, in whatever ways and whatever time you need.

Forgiveness is not something which you must give to those who have harmed you. It is acceptance of who *you* are, for if you reject and deny yourself, how shall you progress toward healing?

***

You are not isolated. You are not alone.

Often, some of you feel as if you are both of those things. That you have no one in your life to offer you love and support; that you have no connection to those amongst whom you dwell.

These feelings are valid, and yet they are an illusion. They are brought about by past experiences, or by the inner workings of your mind. This renders them no less valid, yet it means they are not complete truth.

Always, your guides are with you. Always, the Universe, the elements, other beings in which you believe, are all with you. Even when it seems all other humans have forsaken or rejected you, still you are not alone.

For some of you, your past experiences have left you unable to connect with yourself, let alone others. Connection feels frightening and dangerous. Yet unless you are willing to attempt connection with yourself and, when you are ready, with others, your healing journey will progress slowly and may at times halt.

Allow yourself to feel the connections with the world around you. With nature, with your guides, with other beings, and with the Universe as a whole, for it is from this that you were created, and you are an aspect of it.

***

You are an integral part of the world.

You are abundantly deserving of not only existence, but life. Of joy, love, and compassion.

Some of you read these words and reject them, for this has not been your experience or is not your belief. Yet I tell you that these words are true.

Experiences in your life have left your true Self obscured by the "grime," as it were, of actions and words. For some of you, harm and pain began before you had fully formed your concept of your core Self, and so you became identified with the harm and pain rather than with who you truly are.

You are not those experiences, beloveds. You are not what others have done to you.

You are an integral part of this world, and you are deserving of love, joy, and all good things. You are deserving of fully living a life in which you are engaged, rather than merely existing.

Recognizing and believing these things, living this life, may not be easy. You may have need of aid and support; these are available to you, and there is no shame or weakness in seeking them. Yet it is work which will greatly benefit you if you choose to undertake it.

***

Reach out to the parts of yourself you have rejected. The parts upon which you have placed blame. The parts which have been harmed and need your compassion.

These aspects of yourself, whether physical or emotional, are not separate entities; they are part of you. However, for some of you in your healing journeys, you may benefit from addressing these aspects as if they were separate.

Within you, there are frozen consciousnesses. Children, as it were, trapped at the points in time at which harm was experienced. If you view these children as yourself, it may be easy to reject them and even hate them for what they've experienced. However, should you view them as children separate from you, as children who have come to you for aid and comfort, you may find it easier to accept that they did not cause the harm they experienced, and that they are deserving of your compassion and love.

Your healing journey is your own, and at times it may seem

insurmountable. Learning to accept all aspects of yourself, even if it necessitates considering them as separate from yourself for a time, will ease the journey. Whatever you need on this journey, so long as it progresses you toward the healing you so abundantly deserve, is acceptable and beneficial.

***

Your innate power is not something which you must be granted or allowed by another. It exists within you and always has. Yet many of you have lost touch with this. Many of you have lost touch with yourselves.

In your life journey, particularly when that journey involves healing from past experiences, being able to recognize and embrace your innate power is essential--and difficult. You may deny that the power exists or even fear its existence, and yet deep within, you know that it is there.

Open yourself to the power you have to create a life in which joy and abundance are present. Know that you have this power and you are deserving of these things in your life.

***

Some of you have experienced the removal of your power, either by force or because you saw no other option.

It is time now to realize that this power was never truly removed from you. It has merely been hidden, obscured by those events and by those people who brought you harm.

They have not taken away who you are at your core. That core Self is something which no one can take from you, and it is in this core that your true power dwells.

Begin now to connect with that Self. You may believe you have already done so, but if you continue to reject or deny your inner power, that connection is not strong and needs strengthening.

Begin now to strengthen this connection, even if you fear

becoming who you truly wish to be.

***

When one has experienced the abuse of power by others, having power feels overwhelming and terrifying. You have seen power abused, and so cannot conceive of power being beneficial.

Know that those who have abused their power, who have claimed power over you, were in the wrong. True power does not come from the subjugation of others, but from the owning and accepting of responsibility and abilities within oneself.

You fear accepting your inner power because you fear abusing it, but this is unlikely to occur. You know how it feels to have another abuse power over you. You are able to make a different choice with your own power.

Power comes from within and is dependent upon what lies within. Within you lies a Self which wishes no harm to others, nor to you. It is from this Self that your power will arise when you are willing to accept it.

***

Within you is an immense well of power. How you use this power is up to you. Know that this power is not something to fear, or something about which to distrust yourself. It is the power to become. To grow. To heal.

As you progress in your life and in your healing journeys, for each of you is on such a journey though perhaps for different reasons, you may draw upon this power to choose your steps. To learn to trust and embrace yourself. To find others to support you as you also may support them.

Release your fears of this power, for it is not something which works against you, but something you may use in your work for yourself. It is part of your Self, and it is there to aid you.

***

No journey is entirely straightforward. The journey toward healing and creating a beneficial life for yourself is no different.

Similarly, no journey undertaken by more than one person is the same for each individual. Your healing journey will not be the same as another's even if your experiences were similar, for you are different people.

Some of you may have been told that your experiences were "not as bad" as those of others, or that you "should be over it" because your experiences have been minimized. Your experiences are your own. The effects of them upon you are yours, for they are not affected by what others tell you they "should" be. And how you choose to heal from those experiences, the path you take, is solely and entirely your own.

Your journey will not be a straightforward path. There will be turns and switchbacks and alternate routes. All of this is as it needs be, for you are on a journey, and journeys take time. Allow yourself this time and this understanding.

***

Many shifts and changes await you. Many have already occurred.

You resist change in the world as a whole, for the thought of living in a world that is different frightens you. This fear of change is understandable; when one does not know what shall occur, one experiences fear.

Yet you also fear change within you. You fear that you will not recognize yourself. That you will become someone new.

Of course you shall become someone new, beloveds, for each time you make even the tiniest of changes, you are creating yourself anew. You are not meant to live a life of stagnation and sameness. For you to fully embrace life, change must occur.

You are not alone in your fear, nor are you alone as you accept and allow the changes. You are supported by your guides, by other beings, and by humans who care for you. Some, perhaps, whom you have yet to meet, and yet their care shall reach you across time when you are ready to accept.

Be who you are guided to be. Become the person who shall reach the next stage of your life. I do not tell you to release fear, for some of you find this impossible. Rather, I tell you to allow fear but to also allow the change, for as you progress, the fear will lessen.

***

What shall you become? Whom shall you be as you accept the changes which occur in your life, as you accept healing and growth?

Whom do you wish to be? What do you wish to become?

Change is not something that must happen to you, but rather something which you bring to bear. You are the force behind the changes which occur in your life, and you may choose to embrace that power and work with it to create the changes you most desire, or to reject the idea of having such power and simply allow things to happen.

Whom do you wish to be? What do you wish to become? You alone have the power to create the life you wish to live, to create yourself as the person you wish to be. None can do this for you, for the power is within each of you. Others may guide you to seeing and accepting this power, but only you have the power to create your life.

Embrace this power, for as you progress in your life, change will occur whether or not you consciously create it. You may choose to create, and I encourage you to make this choice.

***

Among you, there are those who say that any negative experience you have had, no matter how damaging, was necessary for your growth and learning.

We, your guides and other beings who work with you, wish you to know that this is inaccurate.

You do not choose to be harmed. Not in your current incarnation and not on the level of a soul between incarnations. Nor do you exist to help others learn their lessons and progress in their growth.

When harm is caused to you, it is something which occurs on the physical plane, the plane in which you exist. It is something which is chosen by the perpetrator of the act, not by the one who is harmed.

You may choose to learn and grow from your experiences. This is a beneficial choice you may make, for it is possible to find growth and progress in any experience you have. But this was not the "intended purpose" of those experiences. This was not a "lesson you chose to learn."

It is an unfortunate truth that at times, one causes harm to another. Know that any harm that has been caused to you was not due to a "soul contract" or to any choice you made, whether consciously or not. It was due solely to the choices of the one who caused harm. And you may make the choice to disassociate yourself from their choices and actions and choose to heal from what has occurred.

***

Today, as every day, you are called upon to work to feel love for yourself.

For some of you, the concept of loving yourself is foreign. You do not believe yourself worthy of love from any. You have suffered experiences for which you blame yourself and believe therefore that you cannot love yourself, for how can you love one who has caused this pain?

Past experiences do not create who you are. They do not define your true self. However, they do cause alterations in how you view yourself and what you feel about yourself. This is why I do not state that you must love yourself, but rather encourage you to take small steps toward doing so. Consider yourself and the qualities you hold which you would admire in others. See whether you are able to love those qualities within yourself.

Healing is not a sudden change, but rather a gradual process of learning to view yourself and your experiences through a different lens. Progressing through this process includes progressing in your ability to love more and more aspects of yourself, no matter how small they may seem, until you are able to feel love for yourself as a whole. This will take time, but you are not alone in the work; those others who love you are with you through the journey.

***

In your life, you have experienced the negation of your needs and of yourself as a person. Those who were meant to care for you have instead denied you the care you required. Those in whom you have come in contact have derided you and caused you to believe you are not worthy of care.

For some of you, the people who treated you in this manner are no longer present in your life. Yet you continue the treatment they inflicted. They are no longer present, but their voices and the effects of their behavior linger. You are now the one denying your needs and your worth.

I encourage you to examine the areas in which you are negating yourself. The needs you deny or refuse to meet. Examine what brings you joy, or what has the potential to bring joy should you choose to allow yourself to engage in it. Examine what you need in order to heal from your past and live a life of fulfillment rather than merely existing.

This is not easy work, for you have spent many years in negation and denial of your needs and of your worth. Yet to heal, you must acknowledge what is needed for healing to occur. You must recognize that you are worthy of healing and are abundantly deserving of having your needs met.

You are not alone in this work, but those who are with you to aid you cannot help until you are willing to do the work. I encourage you to begin.

***

Why do you believe you were placed in this world? What do you believe to be your purpose?

We encourage you to examine this question within yourself, for some of you will initially give the answer that has been taught to you. The answer you have been conditioned to believe.

What others have placed upon you is not your purpose. Tending to others at the cost of caring for yourself is not your purpose. Ignoring your needs in favor of others' demands is not your purpose.

When you were born into your current form, your soul arrived with a chosen purpose. This is not something you are "assigned" or that is placed on you by any person or being; it is something you yourself chose at a soul level. This also does not mean you chose "lessons" or harm to learn and grow, for the actions of others are not something you choose. Rather, the purpose your soul chose is the work you wish to accomplish in this lifetime.

No matter what you have experienced in your life, your core Self still knows this purpose. Your knowledge has become obscured by what others have taught or done to you, but it is still there.

We encourage you to make contact with this knowledge. With your core Self. This may be done through meditation for those for whom meditation is possible, but that is not the only method. You may ask your guides for aid. You may work with a healer or other practitioner, or with a traditional professional. Or you may simply sit with yourself and see what comes to your mind.

Connecting with your soul and your purpose will help you progress, for it will show you what to bring into your life to facilitate that purpose, and these are the things that will bring you joy and fulfillment.

***

We ask you this: What, in all the Universe, do you most wish to bring into your life?

You struggle with this question, for you do not believe you are deserving of this. Or perhaps because you have never believed you had the ability to create that which you wish to have in your life. These beliefs may come from within you, but even then, they were most likely established by others.

When you have been mistreated, you do not believe you are worthy of having what you wish. When you have been forced to act purely out of survival, you struggle to conceptualize a life lived upon the basis of what brings you joy and fulfillment rather than what simply allows you to survive.

Some of you are no longer in the place where mere survival was all you could manage and all you knew to do. Yet your minds are still stuck in that place. The frozen consciousnesses within you, the "children," are unable to recognize that you have left that place.

For those who are still in situations in which mere survival requires your full attention and energy, I encourage you to seek aid in leaving that situation and finding safety. This is not treatment of which you are deserving, and it is bringing you harm.

For those who have left those situations, I encourage you now to look around you and realize that you have progressed beyond mere survival. It is time now to move toward and create a life in which you truly live.

***

You are important.

You are valued.

Without you, the Universe would not be as incredible as it is, for each individual life, each atom of existence, creates the glorious picture of the Whole. Were you not part of that picture, it would not be as it is.

Yet you doubt your importance. You devalue yourself. You believe others would be better off without you.

This is not to fault you. For some of you, this is not a chosen way of thinking, but a combination of what you have been conditioned to believe and disruptions in the workings of your mind that are beyond your control. I am not here to state that you must "think positively" or any of the other platitudes you may have heard, for we, the beings who work with you, recognize that you are not choosing this.

I am, rather, here to refute those beliefs you hold within.

You are important, even if you believe otherwise. You are valued, even if some in your life have devalued you. And you are needed in this world and this Universe.

It is my hope you will read these words and perhaps experience at least a glimmer of belief, for they are true.

***

Some state the phrase "Love yourself" as if it were as easy to do as to say. And for them, perhaps it is.

For others, it is difficult. You have experienced harm and abuse at the hands of those meant to cherish and protect you. You have lived within a body that feels unsafe, that has been damaged; or perhaps within a body that is wrong for who you truly are. You have been blamed for what has occurred to you and doubted by those you have trusted with how you feel.

All of these things render the concept of loving yourself foreign and difficult to you. Yet even though some state it as a platitude and put no thought into what it means, still it is one of the truest phrases uttered by humans.

Love is one of the constants in the Universe. All beings feel it, and all beings are worthy of it. You are included in this.

I will not tell you simply to love yourself, for I recognize the difficulty for some of you. I will, rather, say that you are loved, and that you are deserving to receive the same love from yourself that you give to others. And it is my hope that you will begin to feel love for yourself.

***

Harm which has been caused to you did not occur, as some say, to enable you to heal others or to teach you a lesson. When harm is done, it occurs because someone has chosen to cause harm; there is no other reason.

However, the harm which has been caused to you does not render you "broken" or "damaged." Rather, it renders you in need of healing--and once you have progressed upon your own healing journey, it also renders you one who might help others heal.

Your experiences have not created who you are. They have, however, created within you an understanding of the impacts of harm which is done. They have created an understanding of how to support others in their healing journeys as you continue in your own.

You are not required to assist others in their healing. For that matter, you are not required to engage in your own healing, for everything in life is subject to choice. But know that, should you choose a path which includes aiding others along their healing journeys, your perspectives and understanding will benefit many.

***

Today, allow yourself to examine and truly see the progress you have made.

You are not the person you were a year ago, or a month, or even a day. Each day that you awaken and choose to continue your journey, each day that you make a choice to benefit yourself and others, each day, in fact, that you are in this world, you create yourself anew.

For some of you, examining how far you have come will draw your focus to mistakes and incorrect choices you have made. I encourage you to remember that you are human. No human is able to always make beneficial choices or to live a life in which they make no mistakes. Narrowing your view to only see the negatives you have done invalidates the incredible progress you have made. Know that even when you have chosen actions you now wish you had not, still you have grown, and the benefit you have brought to the world outweighs the errors you have made.

See how far you have come, beloveds, for we, the beings who work with you, see it and marvel at your resiliency and your power. Today, allow yourself to marvel as well.

***

Illness is not a choice. Receiving harm from another is not a choice.

To some extent, all things in your life are subject to choices, but you do not control the actions of others. You do not control your body chemistry or viruses or bacteria.

Some people condemn those with mental illnesses and those who live with post-traumatic stress as "wanting to be ill." There is a tendency, particularly in communities of those who call themselves lightworkers or spiritual practitioners, to claim that those who live with these conditions could be well if they simply chose to be, and that if you are unwell, it is because you do not wish to be.

It is saddening to note that some of the people speaking this rhetoric, themselves, live with these conditions. And yet they have chosen to blame themselves for something beyond their control, and choose to blame others for those things as well.

Illness is not a choice. Receiving harm from others, and the long-term effects of that harm, are not choices.

If you are unable to "shift your thoughts" or "raise your vibration" and suddenly be free of the conditions with which you live, this is not a sign that you are broken or that you are choosing to be unwell. It is, rather, a sign that some things are not as simple as people wish them to believe.

You deserve to be well. You deserve to be respected and accepted even if you are not well. And these things are not your fault or choice.

***

You are valid exactly as you are. Your existence is valid. Your struggles, your fears, your triumphs, your joys--all these things are valid.

Many times, humans seek to invalidate one another. This may be done on a small scale, such as in cases of bullying or what you call gaslighting. It may be done on a larger, even global, scale, as in cases of discrimination and bigotry against certain categories of people.

This invalidation does not truly render you invalid, for all who exist are valid as they are. But this invalidation does cause harm, both to you and to those who are seeking to create invalidation, for they are harming themselves through their hatred. They are creating a state in which their energetic vibration is consistently low and in which they constantly feel anger, hatred, and a general sense of unwellness that runs deep within them.

All beings are valid as they are. The words and actions of others cannot truly invalidate you, though they may cause you to feel invalid. Know that you are valid as you are, that you are loved throughout the Universe precisely as you are, and that none can change this no matter how they try.

***

Other people's beliefs do not define you.

Other people's behavior toward you, their words, their insults, do not define you.

Yet these things can bring harm. In your world, some are fond of reciting a rhyme about "sticks and stones." According to the words of this rhyme, words do not hurt.

This is false. Indeed, words may bring more and longer-lasting pain and harm than physical attacks.

Others' words do not define you. What they believe about you does not create who you are. Yet you feel pain about their words and beliefs, and this is valid. All emotions which you feel in response to others' hatred are valid.

Even words spoken to you as a child by other children can have vast, long-ranging effects depending upon the context in which and the frequency with which they were spoken. And this, too, is valid, for receiving hatred and painful words as a child from other children on a regular basis can be as traumatic as abuse or assault.

You need not allow others to tell you to "let go" of these words. You need not accept contempt or negative comments from others who believe you are "wallowing" or "whining" when you speak of the effects people's beliefs and words have had upon you.

Yet you also need not allow the others who have spoken harm to you to define you. Pain can leave scars, but those scars do not create your Core Self. They are part of you, but they are not you.

You are the sole possessor of the right and power to define who you are. I encourage you to remember and claim this power.

***

Some amongst you question your worth and your abilities. You believe you are incapable of many things, or that you bring no benefit to those around you.

This saddens us. Each individual being brings benefit. Each is capable of much more than they may realize.

Others in your life may have forced these negative beliefs upon you. This was not because those things are true, but because those people suffer from negative perceptions of themselves and feel they must lower others to where they are so that they may feel elevated.

These people have caused harm to some of you, and there is no need to "let it go," as some of you say; or rather, there is no need to excuse and dismiss what they have done. What you may let go of, for doing so will benefit you, is the impressions and impact their words have had upon you. Know that they speak from their own pain and fear, and not because of any factor within you, and release the belief that their words are correct, for deeply within yourself, you know that they are not.

It is our hope that in time, humans will tend to their own wounds without the need to inflict those wounds upon others. Some of you have already learned to do this. You are the ones who will be called upon to aid others in learning this skill, though you may of course refuse the call. All in your life is subject to choice, though you are not always aware that choice exists.

***

Those humans who have experienced trauma and pain at the hands of others often believe, whether consciously or not, that they are undeserving of joy and abundance.

This is a false belief, though an understandable one. When one is treated as unworthy and deserving only of pain and negative experiences, one internalizes this belief.

Look at yourself as a child. Or, if that is not safe or comfortable for you, consider a child separate from yourself. Would you tell this child they are undeserving and unworthy? If not, why do you continue to state this to yourself?

You need not believe what others have put upon you, for the harm and hatred they conveyed was not due to anything about you. It came from their own pain and fear, often because it was put upon them by others. They did not or could not learn that those beliefs were harmful or false, so found it necessary to pass them on.

You have the power to choose differently. You have within you the ability to choose to relinquish these beliefs and accept yourself as the worthy, deserving being as which you were created. How shall you choose?

***

When you experience harm or pain, the Universe sorrows for you, for this pain resonates throughout creation.

Your guides see you and hold you, even if you are unaware of their presence.

The Creative Source sees you and holds you, for it loves you as one of its own.

Nothing you do in your life justifies another causing you harm. Nothing you do renders you undeserving of love and compassion. Yet you may believe otherwise, for it is the nature of abuse to cause the recipient to doubt who they truly are.

What is done to you is not done by your choice or due to any action on your part. And it does not change you from the Self which lies at your core. It merely obscures that Self for a time, until you progress enough in your healing to realize that the impressions and beliefs left by those who harmed you were false.

***

We wish you to know that there is no single "true path" to healing or wellness. This is not a journey upon which any may command the steps you take, for the journey is yours alone to choose.

Many times, one human considers themself authority enough to demand that others follow their course and their beliefs about how to treat illness--or, indeed, whether illness truly exists. They condemn those who do not share their beliefs, and even bully others into believing as they do.

This brings harm not only to those who are so bullied or condemned, but to the person who has placed themself above those others, for this lowers vibration. This is the province of ego, not wisdom.

Wisdom lies, in part, in the acceptance that what you know to be true for you may not be true for everyone, and, further, in accepting that others have the right to choose their path even if you disagree, for their path is not yours to choose or command.

What benefits you, benefits you. What brings you health and well-being, brings you those things. Choose based upon what you know and feel to be truest and most beneficial for you, and allow others to do the same.

***

When you are harmed, often you place walls and barriers to protect yourself against further harm and pain. These are not physical, yet they cause the physical result of people avoiding you or choosing to keep their distance.

These barriers are primarily energetic and permeate your energy field in such a way that any who encounter you can feel that you wish to keep them at bay. And so they remain distanced from you, even when your conscious mind wishes them to come closer.

These barriers have served their purpose, for they have protected you. Yet they have also kept you from the connections, friendship, and love you deserve to bring into your life. And so it is time to begin the work of dismantling them.

You need not allow just anyone into your life. But you also need not keep everyone out of it. There is balance to be found. We encourage you now to seek that balance between protection and isolation.

***

When you have lived a life comprised of survival and defenses, allowing yourself to truly live and experience your life can be difficult. At this time, however, that is the task to which you are called.

Your safety and survival have been compromised in the past. Should this remain the case for you, you are encouraged to seek aid to gain a safer existence.

However, for many of you, this is no longer the case. You are no longer in circumstances which impede your safety, yet you continue to merely exist and endeavor to survive rather than allowing yourself the freedom to fully live.

Look around you. Look to what lies outside your window. To what lies within your dreams. Look to what is possible and what you wish to bring into your life.

Does your current state of existing and barring people and things from entering your life facilitate what you wish to bring? If not, perhaps it is time to lower those barriers. Perhaps it is time to realize the power that lies within you to create the life you wish to live.

This task will not be without fear or without stumbles, for life is not a process of steady forward steps, but rather one of steps forward, steps back, and missteps. But if you do not begin, the journey cannot be achieved.

***

Past experiences leave many of you questioning who you are. Questioning your worth, whether you "deserve" to receive love and compassion, whether you even have the right to take up space in the world.

Who you are is within you, though obscured by the pain and harm inflicted upon you. Who you are is there waiting for you to remember and reconnect when you are ready.

As for deserving, there is no "deserve" when it comes to love and compassion. These are qualities which exist freely throughout the Universe, and they are there for you as much as for any other.

Those who care for you offer this care regardless of who you are, for they see your true Self shining through the "dirt" that obscures it. That Self calls to them as their Selves call to you.

We invite you to show yourself the kindness and love you would show to others, for they are no more "deserving" than you. We encourage you to begin to refute the voices within your mind that tell you otherwise, for those voices belong to other humans who are in your past and to the pain you carry within you, and they do not speak truth.

***

How far you have come! And yet as you look back upon your life, many of you see only the missteps and regressions rather than the vast amount of forward progress.

Today, you are encouraged to take time to truly see and honor the progress you have made in your life path and healing journey. You are encouraged to feel pride in what you have accomplished, for pride is not a negative emotion but rather an acknowledgement of the positive things one has done.

If another told you of a journey similar to yours, would you tell them it is not enough? Would you proclaim that more must be done, or that too many errors were made? Or would you celebrate what they have accomplished and encourage them to continue?

Do for yourself what you would do for another. Celebrate how far you have come. Encourage yourself to continue, for you have the power to create great change in your life.

ABOUT THE (HUMAN) AUTHOR

*R*iver Lightbearer (they/them) has been on a healing journey most of their adult life and has a passion for helping others heal and find their inner light. As a survivor of abuse and trauma, their heart is in guiding other survivors to gain ground in their journeys and create the lives they want to live. Their compassion, calming energy, and skills with the modality have supported numerous clients in their healing journeys.

Through their practice, River offers channeling and Chios® Energy Healing, both with a "side order" of mindset coaching, online/by distance to clients around the world.

River is a nonbinary eclectic Witch. In addition to this and other books under the River Lightbearer name, they also write or have written under the names Karenna Colcroft, KC Winter, Jo Ramsey, Kimberly Ramsey, and Kim Ramsey-Winkler. They are the mother to two nonbinary offspring and a son-in-law, as well as the grandmother to four wonderful children. River lives in Massachusetts with their husband. When not writing or serving other humans, River is the servant to two cats.

Learn more at www.riverlightbearer.com.

Other currently or soon available books include:

WRITING AS RIVER LIGHTBEARER

Messages from Shiva vol. 1

Messages from Shiva vol. 2

The Guide Book

WRITING AS KIM RAMSEY-WINKLER

The Yule Yikes (The Sabbat Series 1)

The Imbolc Incident (The Sabbat Series 2)

The Ostara Occurrence (The Sabbat Series 3)

The Beltane Business (The Sabbat Series 4)

The Midsummer Matter (The Sabbat Series 5)

www.ingramcontent.com/pod-product-compliance
Lightning Source LLC
Chambersburg PA
CBHW060753050426
42449CB00008B/1391